Viva fastrack

BIOLOGY

Elise Masters
B Sc Dip Ed

Viva Books Private Limited
New Delhi • Mumbai • Chennai • Kolkata • Bangalore • Hyderabad

First Indian Edition 2007

VIVA BOOKS PRIVATE LIMITED

- 4737/23 Ansari Road, Daryaganj, New Delhi 110 002
  E-mail: vivadelhi@vivagroupindia.net, Tel. 42242200
- Plot No. 76, Service Industries, Shirvane, Sector 1, Nerul, Navi Mumbai 400 706
  E-mail: vivamumbai@vivagroupindia.net, Tel. 27721273, 27721274
- Jamals Fazal Chambers, 26 Greams Road, Chennai 600 006
  E-mail: vivachennai@vivagroupindia.net, Tel. 28290304, 28294241
- B-103, Jindal Towers, 21/1A/3 Darga Road, Kolkata 700 017
  E-mail: vivakolkata@vivagroupindia.net, Tel. 22836381, 22816713
- 7, Sovereign Park Apartments, 56-58, K. R. Road, Basavanagudi, Bangalore 560 004
  E-mail: vivabangalore@vivagroupindia.net, Tel. 26607409, 26607410
- 101-102 Mughal Marc Apartments, 3-4-637 to 641, Narayanguda, Hyderabad 500 029
  E-mail: vivahyderabad@vivagroupindia.net, Tel. 27564481, 27564482

Published by arrangement with

Pascal Educational Services
655 Parramatta Road
Leichhardt, NSW 2040
Australia

ISBN 81-7649-619-7

Published by Vinod Vasishtha for Viva Books Private Limited, 4737/23, Ansari Road, New Delhi 110 002. Printed and bound at Anand Sons, Delhi.

Contents

Preface

This Pocket Book is written for students studying HSC Biology in NSW. It provides an alphabetical summary of each of the topics and is useful as a checklist during study, or as a reference and glossary.

The chapters correspond to the topics in the course. Chapters 1, 2 and 3 cover compulsory core topics. All five options have been included but only one is necessary for study. Each chapter includes terms and important information for the topic. For easy reference, terms and phrases are listed in alphabetical order. Words in *italics* indicate that more information is included elsewhere in the book. Unless indicated otherwise, the information may be found in the same chapter.

Elise Masters, B Sc, Dip Ed

CHAPTER 1

Maintaining a Balance

acidity See pH.

ADH See *hormones*.

adaptations to temperature Aquatic animals such as fish, which are *ectotherms,* function at *ambient temperature.* Generally they have no special adaptations for temperature control. Whales, seals, dolphins and penguins are *endotherms.* Cool water conducts heat away from their bodies. They have adaptations such as blubber and oil for insulation or they migrate to warm areas. Animals on land have a variety of adaptations to temperature:

- fur and feathers for insulation from heat and cold;
- large surface area : volume ratio to increase absorption of heat in cold habitats and to increase radiation in warm places;
- small SA : vol ratio to reduce absorption of heat in hot habitats and to reduce body heat loss in cold areas;
- light colours to reflect heat, and dark colours to absorb heat;
- low *metabolism* to reduce body heat, or high metabolism to increase body heat;

- extra blood flow to the skin to radiate heat or constricting blood vessels in the skin to reduce heat loss;
- counter-current exchange when heat passes from artery to vein before reaching extremities where heat would be lost; also to prevent hot blood passing into organs and damaging them;
- hibernation (ie. slowing down *metabolism*, lowering of body temperature);
- migration to areas with more favourable temperatures;
- sweating or panting to cool as water evaporates;
- living in burrows or caves, to avoid ambient heat or cold.

Plants are able to regulate *transpiration* which is a cooling mechanism. They may also become dormant, or have hairy or shiny leaves to reflect heat. Surface area of leaves may be reduced to reduce heat absorption in deserts (cactus spines)and to reduce heat loss in cold areas (pine needles).

Radiation and convection are important in heat control.

adaptations to water Many Australian plants have adaptations that allow them to survive in harsh, dry conditions:

- thick waxy cuticle on leaves and stems to reduce water loss;
- sunken *stomates* to reduce water loss;
- opening of *stomates* in the cooler part of the day when water loss is less;
- small leaves. Some leaves have been reduced so much that the stem, which has fewer *stomates*, functions as a leaf;
- hairy or shiny leaves to reflect heat and reduce evaporation;

- leaves curling, enclosing *stomates* to reduce water loss;
- extensive root systems to absorb water;
- leaf and branch arrangement to direct water to roots.

aldosterone See *hormones.*

ambient temperature is the temperature of the surroundings. Temperatures in oceans and seas tend to be stable in the one area throughout the day. This is because water heats and cools very slowly. Temperatures on land have large fluctuations both daily and seasonally. For instance, desert temperatures may range from 0°C to over 50°C in 24 hours. Organisms need mechanisms to enable them to survive fluctuating temperatures. See *adaptations to temperature.*

ammonia See *wastes produced in metabolism.*

arteries See *blood vessels.*

blood is composed of red and white blood cells, platelets and plasma.

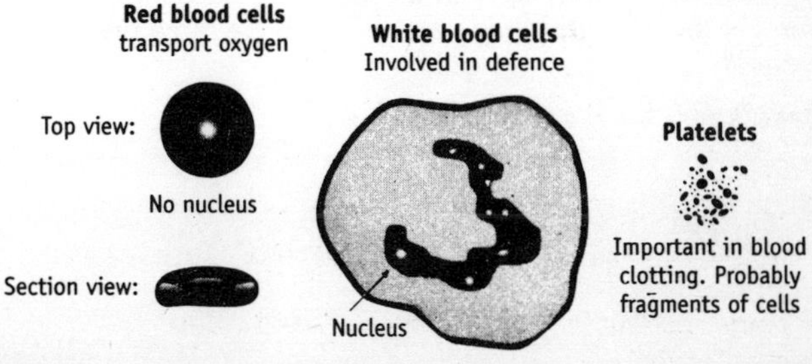

Red blood cells are biconcave and have no nucleus. They contain a red pigment called *haemoglobin*. When *haemoglobin* comes in contact with *oxygen* in the lungs, it attaches to *oxygen* to form oxyhaemoglobin. The red blood cells also carry a small amount of *carbon dioxide* in the form of carbaminohaemoglobin. Plasma is the liquid part of the blood. It is 90% water. Plasma transports *carbon dioxide*. Small amounts are dissolved but most of the *carbon dioxide* is carried as hydrogen carbonate ions. It also carries digested food, lipid globules, salts (ions), urea and hormones.

The composition of blood changes as the blood moves around the body. Blood collects some substances from the tissues and releases others into tissues. For instance, in lungs, *carbon dioxide* leaves the blood while *oxygen* enters. In body tissues the reverse happens and the blood releases food to the cells. Blood collects digested food, vitamins, salts and water from the intestines and collects *urea* from the liver. In the kidney, *urea* and excess salts leave the blood.

blood vessels Substances in the *blood* are transported around the body in blood vessels. There are three types of vessels.

capillaries See *blood vessels*.

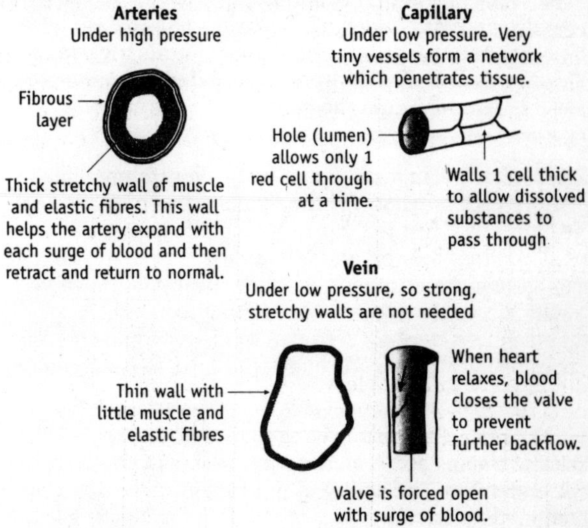

Arteries branch to form a fine network of capillaries penetrating the tissues. The capillaries recombine to form veins. Substances pass into and out of the blood through the thin capillary walls.

carbon dioxide is a metabolic *waste* produced in cells during *respiration*. It is carried by the *blood* to the lungs where it is removed from the body in order to maintain a balanced cell composition.

When the carbon dioxide concentration is high in the *blood*, it makes the blood acidic. This triggers the respiratory control centre in the *brain* to increase breathing rate and remove carbon dioxide.

The acidic *blood* also stimulates the release of *oxygen* from *haemoglobin* to cells. Low *oxygen* in *blood* stimulates the uptake of *oxygen* from the lungs and this triggers release of excess carbon dioxide from the *blood* into the lungs so that it is removed from the body. These mechanisms together maintain a balance of gases in the blood.

ectotherms are animals with a body temperature which changes with the *ambient temperature*. Invertebrates (eg. the house fly), fish (eg. bream), amphibians (eg. the cane toad), and reptiles (eg. the frill-necked lizard) are all ectothermic. An ectotherm produces heat but it is very rapidly lost to the environment so that the animal's temperature is very close to that of the environment. The environment provides the body with heat. See *adaptations to temperature.*

enantiostasis Organisms living in estuaries, bays, inlets, coastal swamps and marshes confront fluctuating salt concentrations. The ability to function in these changing environments is called *enantiostasis*. For instance, gills or kidneys may function differently depending on the salinity; some mangroves excrete salt from their leaves.

endotherms are animals that have a constant body temperature regardless of the temperature changes of the surroundings. Birds (eg. emus) and mammals (eg. red kangaroo) are endotherms. The animal's metabolism provides the body with heat. See *adaptations to temperature.*

enzymes are large protein molecules that speed up chemical reactions in living cells. Each chemical reaction in cells is controlled by its own enzyme. The enzyme is said to be specific for that chemical reaction. The surface of the enzyme molecule has an active site which bonds with the reacting chemical, the substrate. At the end of the reaction the enzyme is unchanged and may be used for further reactions.

Each enzyme works best at a particular or specific acidity or *pH* and temperature. These are known as the optimum pH and temperature. Very low temperatures will inactivate enzymes but this can be reversed and the enzymes will be reactivated. High temperatures will destroy enzymes so that they cannot function again when cooled.

excretion is the removal of *wastes* produced in cellular *metabolism*. In humans, kidneys, lungs and skin are excretory organs. *Carbon dioxide* is produced during *respiration* and is removed by the lungs. *Urea* is removed by the *kidneys* and bladder as urine. Small amounts are removed by the sweat glands in the skin. *Water* is excreted by lungs, *kidneys* and skin.

excretory system. The human system consists of *kidneys*, ureters, bladder and urethra. The kidney's nephrons remove excess salts and water as well as *urea* from the *blood*. See *wastes produced in metabolism*.

feedback mechanisms are required to maintain stable conditions in the body. When the body conditions become unfavourable, information is sent to the control centre to correct this condition. For instance, if the body temperature increases, *receptors* send this information to the brain. The brain sends messages to organs which decrease the temperature. Once the favourable temperature is restored, information is sent to the brain (feedback) to stop the cooling mechanisms.

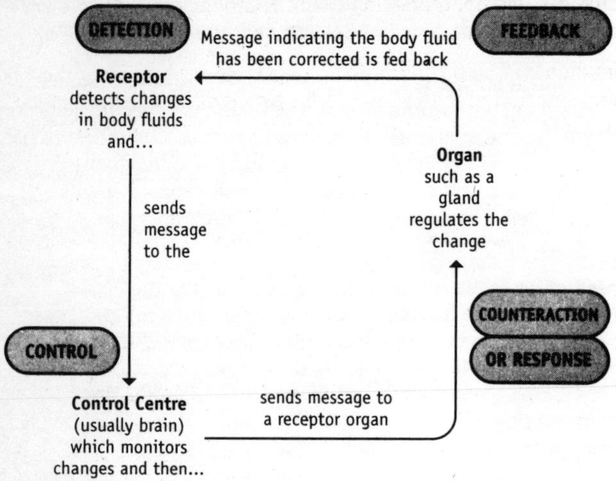

haemoglobin is the pigment found in red *blood* cells. It combines readily with *oxygen* to form oxyhaemoglobin. It also has the capacity to release the *oxygen* readily where it is needed. This red pigment increases the amount of *oxygen* that can be transported.

homeostasis is the process of keeping the internal environment constant. The body fluids must have a stable composition and temperature to remain healthy and to function efficiently. Substances that need regulation are sugars, water, salts, *carbon dioxide*, *oxygen*, *nitrogenous wastes* and other poisonous chemicals. The body is continually monitoring and regulating temperature and the composition of body fluids. *Homeostasis* involves detecting changes and counteracting them. *Feedback mechanisms* are important in this process. See *temperature control.*

hormones The hormone ADH (vasopressin) regulàtes the reabsorption of *water* from kidney *nephrons*. Too little *water* in the *blood* is registered by the hypothalamus in the brain. It produces ADH which causes the *kidneys* to pass more water back into the *blood* and less urine to be produced. If there is too much water the opposite happens.

The hormone aldosterone controls the amount of salt reabsorbed. Low salt concentration in the blood causes production of aldosterone by the adrenal glands. This increases salt reabsorption from the *nephrons* to the *blood*. High salt concentrations cause the opposite reaction.

hypothalamus A region in the brain, located above the pituitary gland. See *temperature control.*

kidney. The human *kidney* excretes nitrogenous waste (*urea*) as well as regulating the ions (salts) in the fluids (*osmoregulation*).

In fish, the gills excrete the nitrogenous *wastes*. The *kidneys* are mainly involved in *osmoregulation.*

In humans, *blood* containing metabolic *wastes*, salts and other small molecules, such as glucose, passes into the *kidney* where it is filtered by *nephrons.* Unwanted substances are passed out of the body via the ureter, bladder and urethra. See *excretion*.

metabolism consists of all the chemical reactions required for the maintenance and functioning of a living organism. *Enzymes* control these reactions. *Enzymes*, and therefore *metabolism*, require certain conditions, eg. *pH* and temperature. The body needs to maintain constant internal conditions for *metabolism* to occur at an optimal level (ie. for the body to reach optimal metabolic efficiency). See *homeostasis.* Metabolic reactions produce *wastes*.

nephron The human *kidney* contains over a million *nephrons* or filtering units. Substances in the *blood* pass into Bowman's capsule and down the tubule. In the tubule, useful substances like *water* and glucose are reabsorbed into the blood while *wastes produced in metabolism* and other unwanted substances pass into the ureter. See *excretory system.*

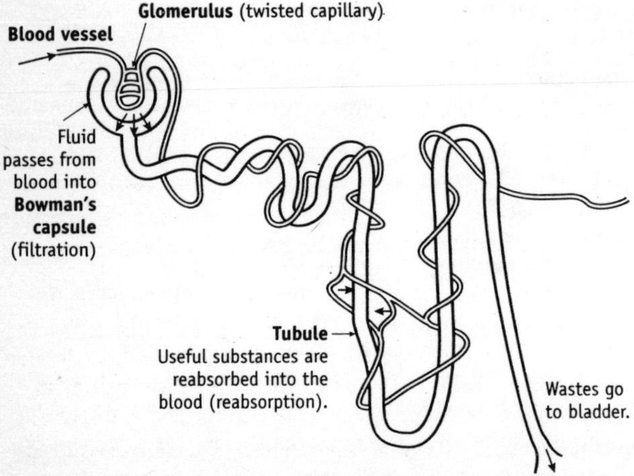

Reabsorption of substances into the blood from the *nephron* tubule involves active and passive *transport*.

Active transport requires energy. It occurs if the substance is too large to pass through the membrane or if the substance is moving against a concentration gradient (from low concentration to high). Amino acids, glucose and salts move by active *transport*. *Water*, a small molecule, moves by *osmosis* which does not require energy and is passive *transport*.

nervous system This is important in *homeostasis* as it is involved in detecting and counteracting changes in an organism. Changes are detected by *receptors* which send electrochemical messages to the brain. The brain sends messages to effector organs (glands and muscles) which counteract the changes.

nitrogenous waste See *wastes produced in metabolism*.

osmosis is the movement of *water* across a semi-permeable membrane. This movement depends on the concentration of fluids inside and outside cells. *Water* moves from the side of the membrane where the concentration of chemicals (solutes) is lower (higher concentration of *water*) to the side where chemical (solute) concentration is higher (lower concentration of *water*). Salt-water fish lose *water* by *osmosis*. To maintain a water balance, they drink large amounts of water, produce very little but concentrated urine, and the gills excrete salts. Freshwater fish are flooded because of *osmosis*. To maintain *water* balance they drink little *water*, produce copious, dilute urine, and actively absorb salts. *Osmosis* is passive *transport*.

osmoregulation maintains the correct concentrations of salts, water and small molecules in the body.

oxygen passes into the *blood* in capillaries in the lungs and is transported by red *blood* cells to cells where it is used in *respiration* to produce energy needed for body functions.

Mammals that live at high altitudes are exposed to low *oxygen* concentrations. Over long periods of time their bodies adjust to ensure that sufficient *oxygen* is provided to the cells. They breathe more deeply, have more red blood cells and *haemoglobin* and have larger hearts to pump more blood.

pH is a measure of acidity and it ranges from 1 to 14.

An acidic substance has a low pH, below 7; a neutral one has a pH of 7. An alkaline substance has a pH above 7. A strong acid has a pH of 1, a strong alkali has a pH of 14.

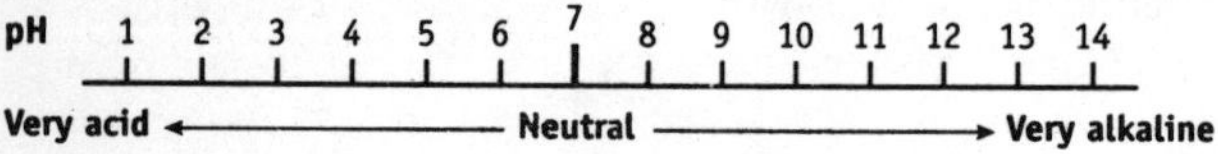

When *carbon dioxide* enters the blood, it combines with the water in the plasma to make carbonic acid:

$$CO_2 + H_2O \rightarrow H_2CO_3$$

Mammals cannot tolerate a change in acidity in the *blood* and have mechanisms to regulate it. See *carbon dioxide.*

phloem is a *transport system* in higher plants. It carries food (glucose) which has been made in photosynthetic cells to tissues where it is stored or used in *respiration*, growth and *metabolism*. Storage cells may be grouped as organs such as fruits (eg. apple), roots (eg. carrots), and seeds (eg.

peas). Other substances such as growth hormones may be carried in the *phloem* as well. Movement of substances in *phloem* is called translocation. The plant needs to supply energy for translocation, so it is referred to as active *transport*. The movement is believed to be caused by a difference in pressure along the *phloem* tubes. Sugars and then water move into the *phloem* in the leaf (the source). They move out at sites where they will be used or stored (the sink). This causes pressure differences which produce a flow in the *phloem*.

TS phloem

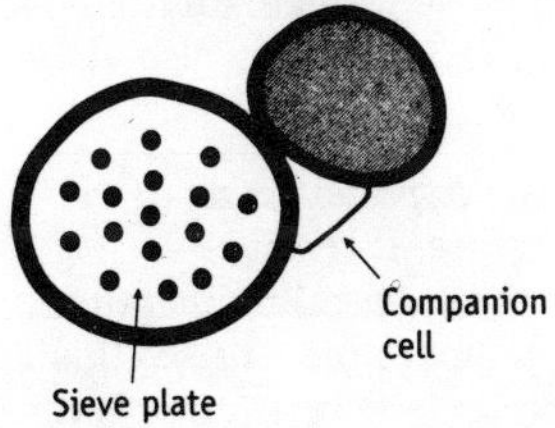

LS phloem

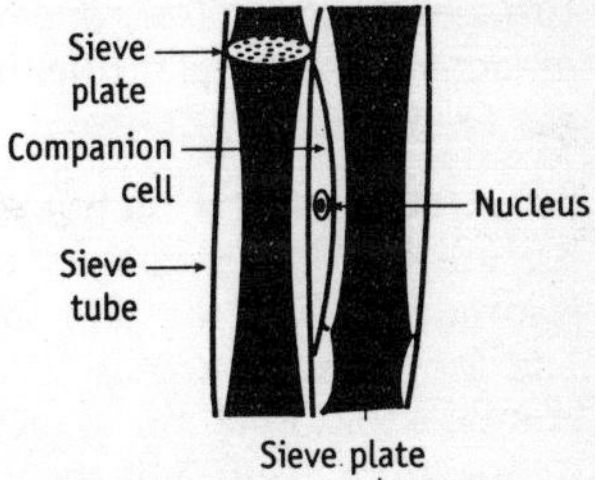

receptors involved in temperature detection are called thermoreceptors. In humans, thermoreceptors are present in the skin and detect external temperature. Internal temperature changes are detected by thermoreceptors in the walls of the *blood vessels* in the *hypothalamus* in the brain.

renal dialysis An artificial *kidney* in a hospital performs the same function as a *kidney* in humans.

respiration (cellular respiration) A complex series of chemical reaction in cells producing energy for use in *metabolism* and cell functioning. The energy is stored in the bonds of ATP. The reaction requires *oxygen* and glucose and produces *water* and *carbon dioxide*, which are removed by *excretion*.

respiratory system In humans this consists of the trachea, bronchi, and lungs containing the bronchioles and alveoli. It is responsible for the passage of *oxygen* into the *blood* and waste *carbon dioxide* and *water* out of the *blood* and body.

stomates These are small pores usually on the lower surface of leaves. They open and close to regulate the flow of *water* from the plant (ie. transpiration). They also allow gas exchange (O_2, CO_2).

temperature control In humans the *hypothalamus* in the brain is the *temperature control* centre. It receives information from the skin about the external temperature, and from the *blood* about tissue temperature. It uses this combined information to regulate body temperature. If the temperature needs adjustment, the *hypothalamus* activates the adrenal and thyroid glands (via the pituitary gland) and the skin, and these organs respond by regulating the temperature. Once the temperature has been adjusted, the *receptors* detect this and messages are fed back to the *nervous system* to stop further adjustment. There is continuous *feedback*.

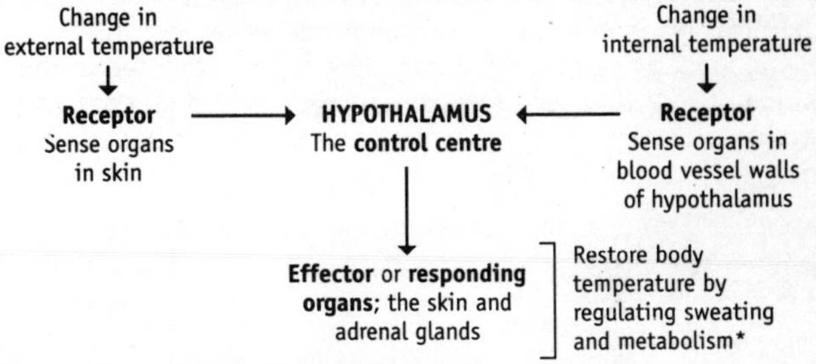

* Once the hypothalamus detects that the temperature has been restored to normal, it switches off 'corrective' messages to sweat glands and adrenal glands.

See *temperature regulation.*

temperature range Life generally exists in temperatures between 0°C and 50°C. However, some bacteria, blue-green algae and crustaceans have been found in temperatures of up to 80°C. Each species has its own favourable *temperature range* and an optimum body temperature for its most efficient functioning. As the body temperature drops, *metabolism* slows and eventually the body becomes inactive. As the body temperature increases, so does *metabolism*. Organisms have an upper temperature limit above which the body cannot function.

temperature regulation If a person becomes too hot or cold, the body responds in a variety of ways:

Human response to overheating	Human response to becoming too cold
Metabolism is reduced. As a result less heat is produced.	Metabolism is increased. This produces more heat.
Sweating: evaporation has a cooling effect as it takes heat from the body.	Shivering: muscles contract to produce heat.
Blood vessels in the skin dilate (become larger). This allows blood to bring more heat to the surface to be radiated from the body.	Blood vessels in the skin constrict. This keeps blood and warmth deep in the tissues so that heat cannot be lost through the skin.
Hairs remain flat, decreasing the insulating layer of air.	Hairs stand up to trap a layer of air which insulates the body and keeps in the warmth.**

** This is rather useless in modern humans as they have little body hair.

translocation is the movement of substances in the *phloem*.

transpiration. This is loss of water from plant surfaces, usually the leaves. *Water*, transported to the leaves by *xylem*, evaporates through the *stomates*. This has a cooling effect on the plant. As water moves upwards in the xylem, minerals are carried to cells.

transport. Active *transport* requires energy to be supplied by the organism (eg. sugar uptake into cells); passive *transport* does not and happens spontaneously (eg. *osmosis*).

transport systems. Substances needed by cells and removed from them are carried by transport systems. Transport systems assist in *homeostasis* by maintaining a nutrient – *waste* balance and an *oxygen – carbon dioxide* balance in the tissues. In animals substances are carried by the red *blood* cells and plasma in *blood*. In plants they are carried by *xylem* and *phloem*.

urea is a metabolic *waste* produced in the liver during the breakdown of excess amino acids in mammals and some other animals. It is removed from the body by the *excretory system*.

uric acid See *wastes produced in metabolism*.

vasopressin See *hormones*.

veins See *blood vessels*.

water All living things need *water*. It is a solvent for chemical reactions.The water in the body contains substances (ions and metabolites) needed for chemical reactions. The organism needs to maintain a particular concentration of these substances for it to work properly. *Kidneys* regulate the composition of the body fluids to ensure water balance and correct concentrations.

wastes produced in metabolism (ie. nitrogenous wastes) are poisonous (toxic) and are removed from the human body by lungs, *kidneys* and skin in *excretion*. Different animals excrete different *wastes*. For instance, when protein is broken down or deaminated, ammonia is formed. It is very toxic and needs to be removed rapidly.

Fish excrete ammonia, mainly through the gills. It dissolves readily in water.

Mammals convert the ammonia to *urea* which is less toxic. *Urea* is soluble. It dissolves in water to form urine.

Reptiles, birds and insects convert ammonia to *uric acid* which is not very soluble and is non-toxic. *Uric acid* is solid, so animals producing it as a waste lose less water from the body.

xylem. This is tissue in higher plants that carries *water* and dissolved minerals from the roots to the leaves. It is composed of dead, hollow cells with strong lignin walls. *Xylem* is made up of vessels and tracheids, which transport the water, and fibres which give support.

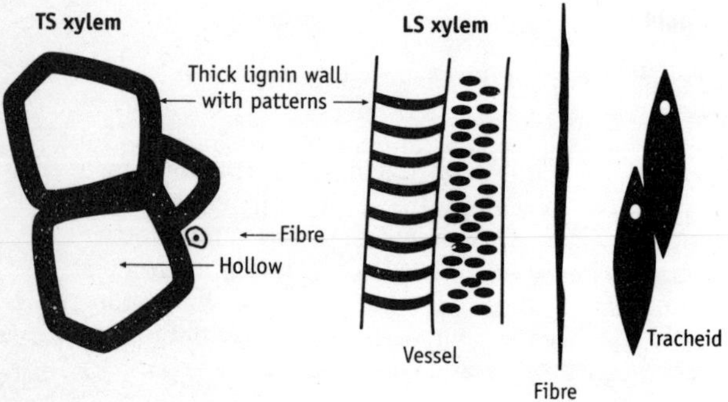

Movement of *water* in the *xylem* is caused by:

- *transpiration* pull; water evaporates from the leaves pulling more water behind it. Cohesive forces between the water molecules hold the water column together;
- capillarity; the adhesive forces between the *xylem* walls and the water pull the water up the fine *xylem* tubes;
- osmotic pressure; pressure is set up in the roots due to the osmotic gradient caused by different concentrations in the cells. See *osmosis*.

The sun's energy is needed for this movement. Energy is not supplied by the plant, so it is passive *transport*.

CHAPTER 2

Blueprint of Life

A: EVOLUTION

adaptive radiation. Organisms of the same species, isolated in different environments, may evolve to form new species. This is called *adaptive radiation* or divergent evolution. *Adaptive radiation* occurs as a result of isolation and adaptation, by *natural selection*, to different environments. See *comparative anatomy.*

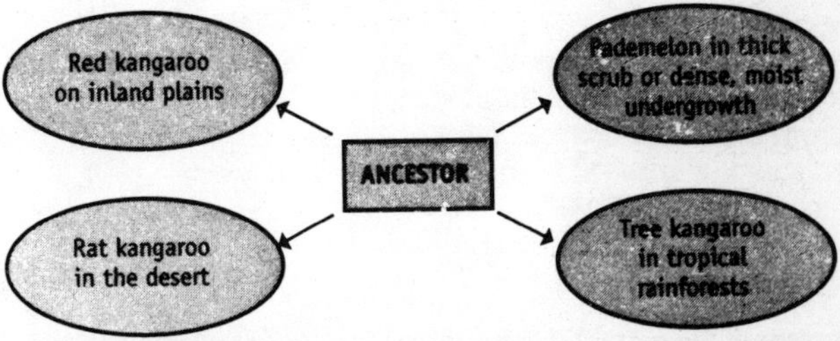

biochemistry is the study of chemical structures and reactions in living things. Cells throughout the different kingdoms of living organisms have similar basic chemistry. Studies and comparisons of chemicals such as proteins, (eg. enzymes) and DNA are used to determine evolutionary relationships. These chemicals will be very similar in two closely related species. Distantly related species will have more differences in chemical structure. For instance, amino acid sequences in haemoglobin (a protein in blood) are very similar in chimpanzees and gorillas, but are different in the more distantly related monkeys. Similarly the base sequences in DNA may be compared and used to determine relationships. Advances in technology involving DNA—hybridisation, protein analysis, and immunological techniques—have provided new information on evolutionary relationships. See *Chapter 7, Option, The Human Story.*

biogeography is the study of the geographical distribution of species and their dispersal from their original site. It provides evidence for *evolution.* Australian mammals are different from other mammals; this suggests that they have evolved separately. Their ancestors were isolated from other mammals when Australia was separated from the other land masses. This freed them of competition with and predation from the better adapted placental mammals. They have adapted by *natural selection* to their own special environment, and so are unique (eg. marsupials thrive only in Australia. In the past they were displaced in other continents).

common ancestry Species which are very similar have evolved from the same common ancestor. As a result of divergent evolution that ancestor gave rise to the similar species.

comparative anatomy supports the theory of *evolution.* The limbs of vertebrates, called pentadactyl (five finger) limbs, show a common pattern and similar structure. This indicates common ancestry. Many vertebrate limbs appear different because they have been adapted for particular environments (eg. some have been modified for flying (eg. bats) and others for swimming (eg. whales)). This is an example of divergent evolution or *adaptive radiation*.

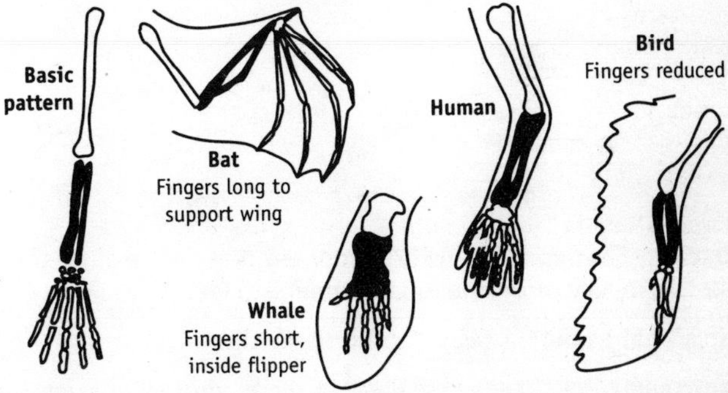

comparative embryology supports supports the theory of *evolution*. Early embryos of vertebrates are very similar; this suggests that they have evolved from a common ancestor.

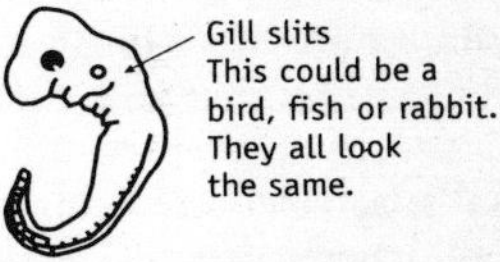

competition for food, shelter, water, and a mate, may lead to *evolution*. Darwin's finches on the Galapagos Islands provide an example. There are 14 different species, each with different beaks and diets; Darwin believed they were from a common ancestor and that those that survived in each habitat were most suited to the food type.

convergent evolution Different species of organisms in similar environments may evolve to look the same. For instance, the shark (a fish) and the dolphin (a mammal) appear similar but are only distantly related. They both have structural characteristics suited to aquatic life (eg. fins/flippers, streamlined body). This is called *convergent evolution*.

Both have streamlined body and flippers/fins.

Darwin, Charles (1809–1882) proposed that the mechanism for the theory of evolution is *natural selection*.

divergent evolution See *adaptive radiation*.

environmental changes Changes in the environment may bring about *evolution*. Those organisms best suited to the change are more likely to survive, breed and pass on genes for features that help them survive. The changes may be chemical or physical. Chemical changes include change in salts, acidity, pollutants or pesticides in the environment (eg. insects exposed to DDT. The more resistant insects survived to breed and pass on their 'resistance' genes. New generations of insects have evolved with a resistance to DDT.). Physical changes that may impact on the evolution of organisms include temperature, moisture and light (eg. plants able to photosynthesise in low light will grow in environments where light is poor. Plants such as lianas have evolved; they can climb over other plants to reach light.

Animals and plants in Australia have evolved characteristics that enable them to survive hot, dry conditions).

evidence for evolution is provided by *palaeontology, biogeography, comparative embryology,* comparative anatomy and *biochemistry.*

evolution is the development of new varieties of organisms from pre-existing organisms, over millions of years. Charles Darwin and Alfred Wallace, in the mid–19th century, put forward the theory of *natural selection* to explain the occurrence of *evolution. Environmental changes* and *competition* for resources may affect *evolution.* Darwin suggested that *evolution* is a gradual process where changes are small and slow. Compare with *punctuated equilibrium.*

fossils See *palaeontology* and *transitional forms.*

historical development of the theory of evclution. Many people contributed to the present ideas on *evolution.*

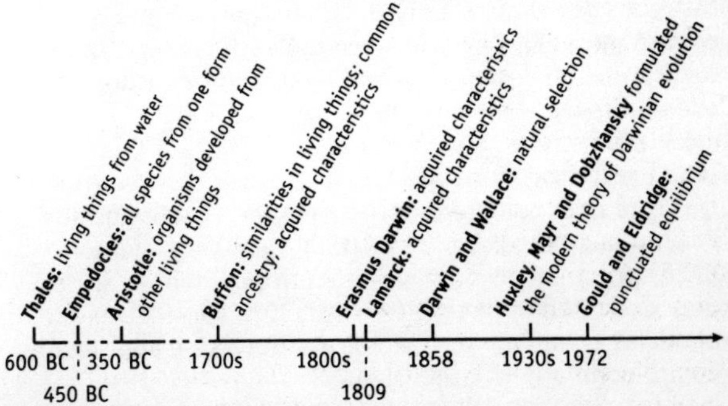

It was speculated by the ancient Greeks, but they could not suggest a mechanism. Lamarck (1810) put forward the idea that using body parts strengthens them, whereas disuse causes them to disappear. He believed these features, which had been acquired by use, could be inherited by offspring. Wallace and Darwin (1858) suggested a possible mechanism: variation of a species allowed *natural selection* where only the fittest survived to pass on their successful characteristics.

natural selection is an explanation proposed by Darwin and Wallace to explain how *evolution* occurs. Organisms of a species have variations and if there are dramatic *environmental changes*, many individuals may die, while others have varying degrees of tolerance to the changes. Those best suited to the environment will survive. This is referred to as 'survival of the fittest'. If this 'tolerance' is in the genes, then the characteristic may be inherited by the offspring. Tolerance for the environmental change will increase the population.

Natural selection is clearly illustrated by changes in the peppered moths in England since the 19th century. In pre-industrial England, the trees had light coloured trunks. Most of the moths were speckled light grey and were camouflaged so the birds could not find and eat them. During the industrial revolution, soot made the tree trunks darker; the light coloured moths were then eaten and the dark ones survived. They passed on their 'dark' genes to their offspring, so eventually the moth populations were mainly dark. Today there is less pollution so the trees are light again. Light coloured moths are surviving and light coloured populations are evolving.

Organisms may build up a genetic resistance to chemicals by *natural selection*. For instance, pests become resistant to pesticides and bacteria become resistant to antibiotics.

palaeontology is the study of fossils. Fossils are the remains or traces of ancient life. They support the theory of *evolution*. Fossils show that organisms in the past were different from modern day organisms and they indicate changes or trends that have occurred. Some fossils show *transitional forms* of life.

punctuated equilibrium In the 1970s the theory of punctuated equilibrium was proposed by Gould and Eldridge. This theory indicates that *fossils* reveal long periods of time when evolutionary development was stable and in equilibrium, and then short periods of rapid change to produce new species. Evolution occurs when there is sudden environmental change. Because *evolution* occurs in short bursts, there is insufficient time for fossil formation; this explains the lack of transitional forms and the incomplete fossil record. Darwin's theory of *evolution* by *natural selection* suggests that species evolve gradually by developing characteristics in response to selective pressures; eg. the fossil record of the horse shows *evolution* occurring gradually over a very long period of time. Possibly both mechanisms occur to produce new species.

transitional forms or fossils Fossils like archaeopteryx and the lobe-finned fish are transitional or intermediate forms. Archaeopteryx is a fossil that has both bird and reptile features. It suggests that birds may have come from reptiles. Lobe-finned fish have lungs, and bones in their fins providing support and allowing them to walk. These and other structural characteristics such as skull bones and teeth resemble those of primitive amphibians. They suggest a possible ancestry of land animals.

The *evolution* of the horse, camel and elephant has been traced through fossils, which provide almost complete records and show changes that have occurred. Early forms of the horse were dog-size, with pointed teeth and four toes, while present-day horses have flat-ridged teeth and hooves.

variation Organisms of the same species are all different from each other. Variation between organisms of the same species is necessary for the process of *natural selection* and *evolution*. See *Chapter 2, Blueprint of Life — B Heredity and DNA*: *variation in offspring.*

CHAPTER 2

Blueprint of Life

B: Heredity and DNA

allele Genes occur in pairs (eg. Tt). Each gene in the pair is referred to as an *allele*. They exist in the same position on homologous *chromosomes*.

antibiotic resistance Some bacteria have become resistant to antibiotics by *natural selection*. As a result, antibiotics are not effective in controlling those bacterial diseases.

artificial insemination See *selective breeding*.

artificial pollination See *selective breeding*.

Beadle and Tatum In the 1940s, George Beadle and Edward Tatum put forward the hypothesis that one *gene* is responsible for the development of one polypeptide, an amino acid chain essential to the structure and function of living things. *Proteins* are made of one or more polypeptides.

biodiversity Reproductive technology and genetic engineering may interfere with the variety of organisms or *biodiversity* (eg. selective breeding will reduce the number of breeds of livestock; genetically modified crops which are resistant to disease will reduce the types of cereal plants. Those with unwanted characteristics will die out.). Variation is needed for *evolution*, which is important in a changing environment. *Gene* banks have been set up to help maintain the diversity of organisms on Earth.

Boveri and Sutton At the beginning of the 20th century, Theodor Boveri and Walter Sutton carried out investigations on *chromosomes* and pointed out the relationships between *meiosis* and Mendelism. The work of both these men contributed to The Chromosome Theory of Inheritance. They showed that *chromosomes*, in *meiosis*, have a parallel behaviour to Mendel's factors or *genes*.

- In *meiosis*, only one *chromosome* of the homologous pair passes into each *gamete*. This supports Mendel's law of segregation that factors (*genes*) occur in pairs and separate into different *gametes*.
- In *meiosis*, two pairs of homologous *chromosomes* separate independently of each other. Mendel's law of independent assortment states that two different types of *genes* (eg. Aa and Bb) are inherited independently (ie. the offspring may receive AB or Ab or aB or ab).

chromosomes are thread-like structures found in the nucleus of a cell. They are composed of *DNA* (deoxyribonucleic acid) coiled around a *protein* core and contain the *genes*.

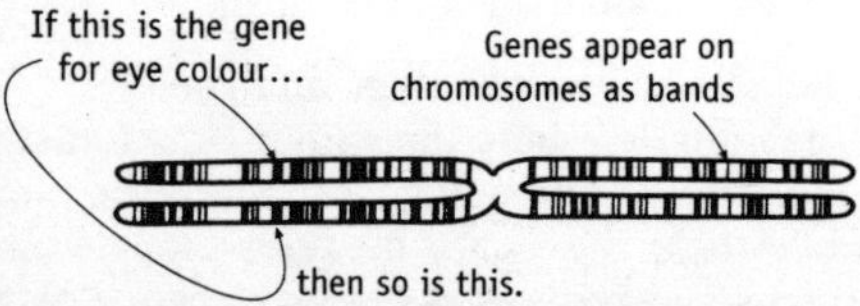

cloning A clone is an identical copy of an organism. Gardeners have been cloning plants for years by growing plants from cuttings and grafts. Other methods of cloning are tissue culture, embryo twinning and nuclear transfer techniques. Tissue culture is commonly used in plants to produce thousands of offspring. Small pieces of plant tissue are grown on a sterile medium. The callus tissue formed is then cultured for future use, or split to form many new plants. Animals are cloned by embryo twinning. The embryo is split at a very early stage and the development of each new, identical half is allowed to proceed. Cloning is also done by nuclear transfer techniques. A mature cell is combined with an egg cell (with its nucleus removed) of another animal. The resulting embryo is implanted into an animal for development. The new animal formed is genetically identical to the donor of the mature cell.

codominance A hybrid *genotype* (eg. Tt) usually shows the dominant characteristic. If both genes are dominant, the individuals will show both characteristics, and the *genes* are referred to as *codominant*. For instance, a red cow crossed with a white bull will produce roan calves, which have both red and white hairs. RR × WW produce offspring RW. A cross between two roan animals will produce 1 red : 2 roan : 1 white.

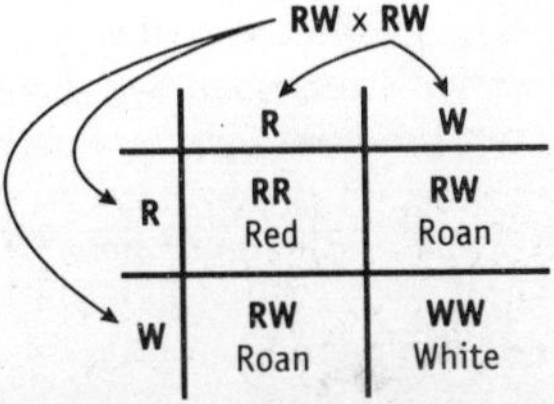

Codominant cross

crossing over occurs when a piece of chromosome swaps with a similar piece on its pair during *meiosis*. This increases genetic variation.

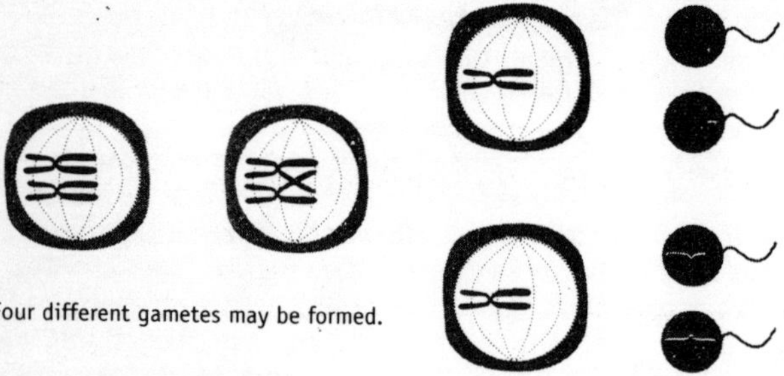

Four different gametes may be formed.

diploid number of chromosomes See *haploid number.*

DNA (deoxyribonucleic acid). *Chromosomes* are composed of DNA and they contain the genetic code. A DNA molecule is made of two strands (*polynucleotides*) twisted around each other in the form of a double helix. The strands are made up of sugars (called deoxyribose), phosphates and four different bases. The base called adenine will only pair with thymine, and cytosine will only pair with guanine. The *genes* are arranged in sequence along the *polynucleotide* strand and are made up of a series of bases. The order of the bases along a *polynucleotide* strand provides the code for the synthesis of a specific *protein*. When new cells are formed, new DNA must also be made for these new cells. This process is called *DNA replication*. DNA and the genetic code are passed on to the next generation by *gametes* (eggs and sperm) which are formed by *meiosis* in advanced organisms.

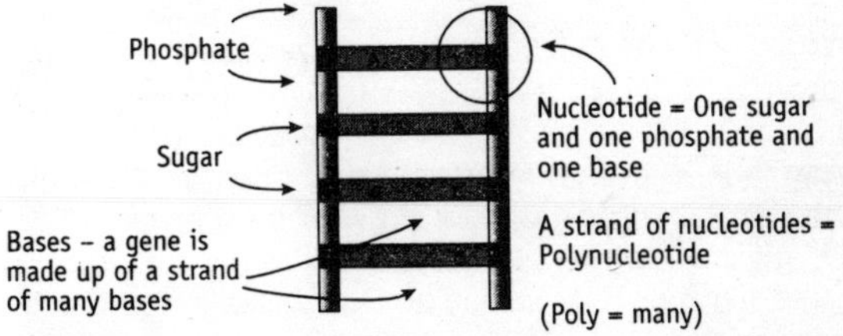

DNA replication When new cells are formed, new *DNA* must also be made for these new cells. This process is called replication, and the new *DNA* is identical to that in the original cells. *DNA* and the genetic code are passed on to the next generation in *gametes*, formed in *meiosis* in most higher organisms.

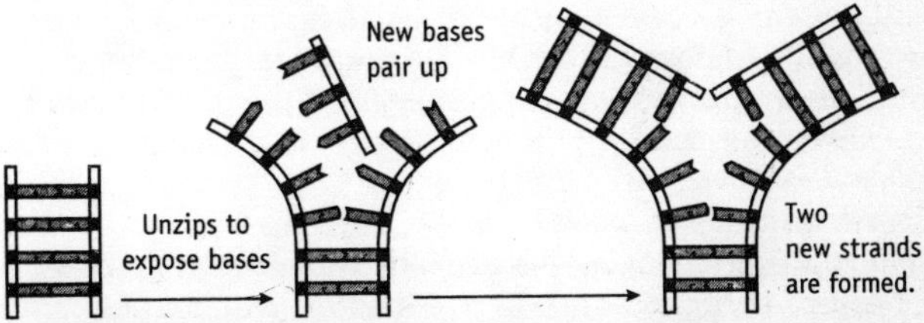

dominant gene When an individual is *heterozygous*, the *phenotype* and its expressed *gene* are referred to as dominant (eg. if an organism has alleles for yellow and green but appears yellow, then the yellow *gene* is dominant). It is usually represented by an upper case letter (Y). The hidden or masked characteristic and its *gene* are recessive and given a lower case letter (y).

environment and genes Both *genes* and the *environment* contribute to the characteristics (phenotype) of an individual. The *genes* provide the potential for a characteristic and the *environment* influences the expression of the *genes*. For instance, a girl may have *genes* for dark hair but environmental factors, such as the sun, may have caused her hair to bleach. The Himalayan rabbit has black ears, feet and tail in winter. In warmer temperatures the hair on these extremities is pale. In humans, studies of twins are used to determine the contribution of the *genes* and the *environment* to a person's characteristics.

ethical issues about cloning and genetic engineering There are a number of concerns about the use of *cloning* and *genetic engineering*. For instance:

- If *genes* are incorporated in the sex cells, then the new *gene* can be passed on to the children; do we have the right to impose genetic change on future generations?
- *Genetic engineering* changes organisms; will this upset the balance of nature? Will new organisms get out of control and interfere with others?
- Are genetically modified foods safe to eat?
- People are changing the diversity (numbers of different types) of organisms. Will this interfere with natural *evolution*?

family tree See *pedigree*.

gamete A reproductive cell; ovum in females and sperm in males. Gametes contain the *haploid number* of chromosomes (ie. half the number found in body cells or one set of *chromosomes*). This reduction of chromosome number, and the formation of gametes, occur during *meiosis*. *Gametes* combine in the process of fertilisation.

gene A unit of heredity, found on *chromosomes* and made up of a series of bases on the *DNA* molecule. A *gene* making up a pair is known as an *allele*.

genetic code See *DNA* and *protein synthesis*.

genetic engineering In recent years, scientists have developed the process of *genetic engineering* in which the actual *genes* of an organism may be altered and new *genes* may be added to the individual. A transgenic organism is one that has received genetic material from another organism and can pass this *DNA* onto its offspring (eg. strawberries containing a fish *gene* so that they can grow in cold climates).

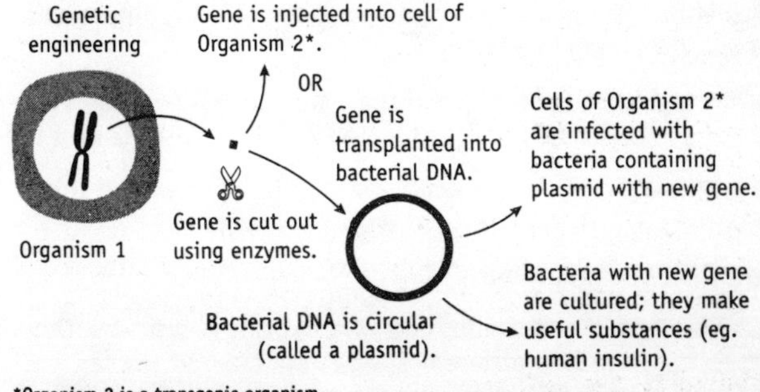

*Organism 2 is a transgenic organism.

Genetic engineering may provide many benefits, such as the production of disease– or frost-resistant crops; fruits which remain fresh; high yielding crops; medicines (eg. insulin, growth hormones and antibiotics); bacteria which can 'eat' oil slicks or manufacture substances (eg. plastics, fuel or vitamins). Research into *gene* therapy has provided a cure for the immunodeficiency disease SCIDS, and continuing research will possibly provide cures for diseases such as cystic fibrosis.

genotype indicates the *genes* present. For instance if T represents the *gene* for tall and t for short, then a plant may have a genotype of TT, Tt or tt. *Gametes* have a *genotype* of T or t.

haploid number This is the number of *chromosomes* found in *gamete* cells produced by *meiosis*. These cells have half the number found in other body cells. Body or somatic cells have the full complement of *chromosomes* (ie. 2 sets; every *chromosome* has a pair partner) known as the diploid number. In humans the *haploid number* is 23 and the *diploid number* is 46. Ova and sperm have 23 chromosomes, while other body cells have 46.

heterozygous or hybrid describes a genotype where the two alleles are different (eg. Tt). Compare with *homozygous*.

homozygous describes a genotype that has two alleles the same (eg. TT or tt). Compare with *heterozygous*.

hybrid See *heterozygous*.

hybridisation is the production of a hybrid. A *hybrid* is the offspring when two different species are crossed (eg. a horse crossed with a donkey produces a mule). Compare with *heterozygous*.

insecticide resistance Through overuse, some insect species have become tolerant to pesticides by *natural selection* and so are not killed by them. This is an example of evolution in modern times.

meiosis is cell division producing *gametes.* During *meiosis* the diploid number of *chromosomes* is halved, producing four *haploid* gametes. *Gametes* become different during *meiosis* as a result of *random segregation* and *crossing over.*

Mendel, Gregor (1822–1884) Gregor Mendel carried out carefully controlled breeding experiments on common pea plants to explain how characteristics are inherited. Pea plants were a good choice as they were available in pure-breeding varieties, they were easy to grow and quick to breed. The flower structure made it easy to control pollination and breeding, and the plants had easy-to-view characteristics. The significance of Mendel's work was not appreciated or understood until 1900, 16 years after his death. Knowledge of cells was poor, and *genes* and *chromosomes* were unknown. His research and principles were so precise that they were later recognised as Mendel's Laws of Inheritance.

Mendel's experiments Mendel examined 7 different characteristics or traits (including seed shape, pea colour and plant height) and found that the offspring were produced in predictable ratios. For instance, when he crossed pure-breeding tall plants with short ones, all the plants in the first generation (F_1) appeared tall; the short trait was masked in this generation but reappeared in later generations (F_2).

In the second generation the new plants appeared in a ratio of 3 tall : 1 short. A cross involving one trait or one pair of genes is known as a *monohybrid cross.*

To explain these results Mendel proposed a set of rules:

- Each characteristic is controlled by two factors (now known as *genes*) (eg. T tall, t short).
- Every body cell has two factors for one characteristic (ie. TT, Tt or tt for height).
- Each *gamete* (ie. ovum or sperm) will receive only one of these factors.
- Fertilisation brings factor pairs together again.
- When an individual is a *hybrid* (Tt), the characteristic that appears, or is expressed, is *dominant*. The characteristic that is hidden is *recessive*.

monohybrid cross A cross involving one characteristic or one pair of *genes* is known as a *monohybrid cross*. The ratio of the offspring produced by breeding two hybrids (Tt × Tt) (eg. TT × Tt, Tt × Tt)is 3 dominant : 1 recessive and may be shown in a Punnett square:

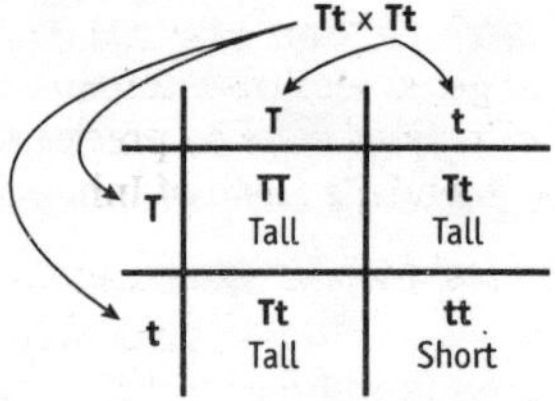

Monohybrid cross

Morgan, Thomas In 1904 Thomas Morgan introduced the idea of sex-linked *genes* as a result of breeding experiments with fruit flies called *Drosophila*. Normal, wild-type fruit flies have red eyes which are produced by a dominant *gene*. White-eye flies are mutants and the characteristic is caused by a recessive *gene*. When Morgan crossed red-eyed male flies with white-eyed females, he did not obtain Mendel's 3:1 ratio in the second generation, because red- and white-eye *genes* are inherited with the X *chromosome*. See *sex chromosomes*.

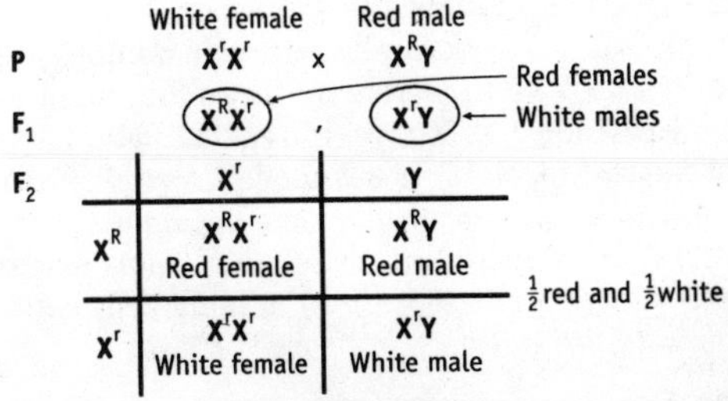

Sex–linked cross

mutagen A factor causing *mutation*.

mutation is a change in the DNA of an organism. It increases *variation* in populations by introducing new *alleles*. Mutations or changes in the *genes* occur if the bases in the DNA are in the 'wrong order'.

Gene mutation	Error in base code
substitution	incorrect base
deletion	base missing
insertion	extra base
inversion	base triplet back to front

The order of the bases determines the order of the amino acids in the protein to be produced. If there is a change in the bases, then a different amino acid will be incorporated in the protein, hence altering the protein formed. This may affect the chemical activity of the cell (eg. if the mutated protein is an enzyme essential for a particular chemical reaction). See *protein synthesis*. Mutations also occur if there is an incorrect number of *chromosomes*.

Mutations may occur naturally but their number may be increased by exposure to factors in the environment called *mutagens*. Radiation (eg. X-rays, ultraviolet light, gamma rays from nuclear reactors) is a *mutagen*. Certain chemicals are also *mutagens* (eg. asbestos, some dyes and preservatives, nicotine and benzene). *Mutations* occurring in sex cells may be inherited; those in body cells cannot. Most mutations are harmful.

nucleotide See *polynucleotide*.

pedigrees or family trees are used to describe the ways in which characteristics are inherited and to follow a particular characteristic through generations.

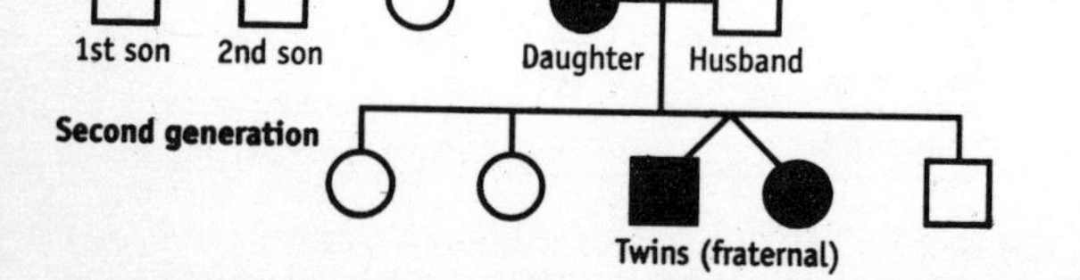

phenotype is the appearance of an organism due to the genes present. If T represents the *gene* for tall, and t the gene for short, an organism with *genes* TT or Tt will have a *phenotype* of tall; tt will appear short. The *phenotype* can also be influenced by the environment. See *environment and genes.*

polynucleotide A chain of nucleotides. Each nucleotide is formed from a base, sugar and phosphate. *DNA* and *RNA* are made up of polynucleotide strands.

polypeptide See *protein and polypeptide synthesis.*

protein and polypeptide synthesis *Proteins* and *polypeptides* are the building materials of cells, tissues and enzymes. They are made up of long chains of amino acids. DNA controls the type of *protein* made by cells. The order of the bases on the DNA molecule provides a code for the amino acids and hence the proteins to be formed.

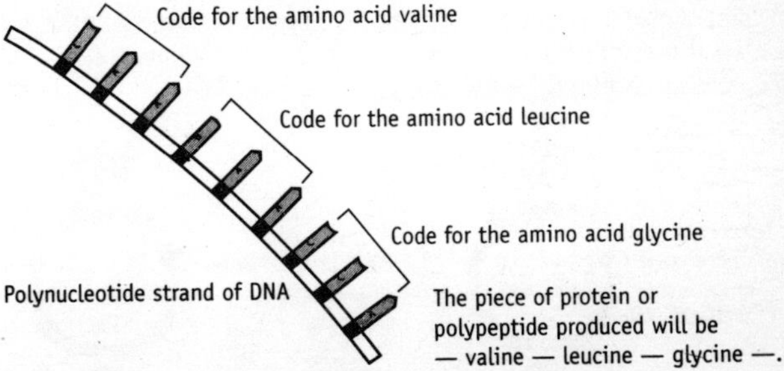

For *proteins* to be made, the DNA code is taken to ribosomes by messenger *RNA* (mRNA). Amino acids in the cytoplasm are taken to the ribosomes by transfer *RNA* (tRNA) which links with the messenger *RNA* to form *protein*.

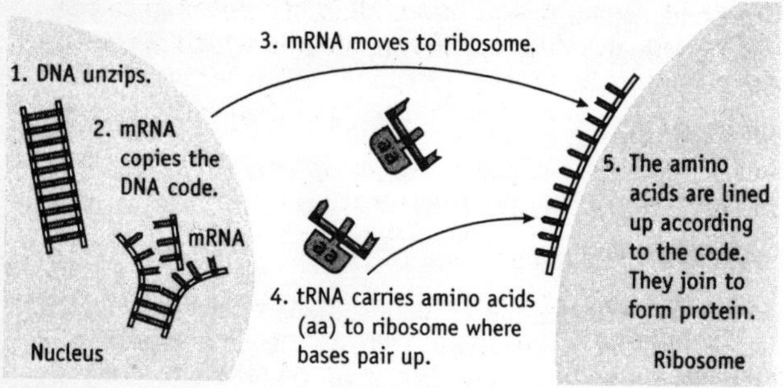

Punnett square See *monohybrid cross.*

random segregation Genetic *variation* in *meiosis* occurs as a result of *random segregation* or independent assortment of *chromosome* pairs and their *genes*. The *chromosomes* line up along the equator of the spindle and move to new cells (*gametes*) independently of other *chromosomes*.

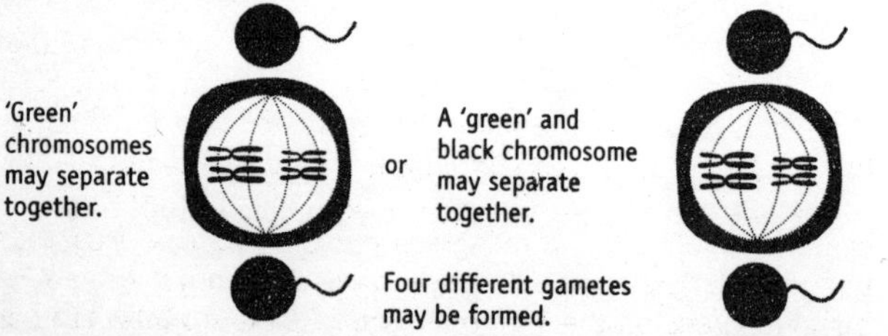

See *meiosis.*

recessive gene See *dominant gene.*

RNA (ribonucleic acid) is a single-stranded molecule similar to a *DNA polynucleotide* strand. It is composed of sugars and phosphates and four bases: adenine which pairs with uracil (not thymine, as in the *DNA* molecule) and cytosine which pairs with guanine. mRNA and tRNA are involved in *protein synthesis*.

selective breeding has been carried out for over 2000 years to improve produce such as fruits, vegetables and cereal crops. Artificial insemination is used to improve stock (eg. cattle, sheep). In this process, semen containing sperm is removed from the male and placed in the female, using a catheter. Breeding of plants may be improved by artificial pollination, where humans control which particular plants are bred. Traditional methods of *selective breeding* to produce improved offspring are slow and the results are often unpredictable. Techniques such as *cloning* and *genetic engineering* are faster and more reliable in producing the desired result.

sex chromosomes The gender of living things is determined by the *sex chromosomes*. In male mammals the *sex chromosomes* are XY. In females they are XX. All ova contain one X *chromosome,* while sperm may contain an X or a Y. *Genes* which are on the same chromosome are said to be linked. Those on the sex *chromosomes* are sex-linked.

Examples of sex-linked genes in humans are those that cause haemophilia and red–green colourblindness. Most sex-linked genes are on the X *chromosome* and do not have a matching *gene* on the Y *chromosome.* A colourblind man has the genotype X^c Y. He will be colourblind even though the *gene* is recessive because there is no dominant gene on the Y to mask its effects. A colourblind woman has the genotype X^cX^c.

Women pass on their sex-linked genes to both sons and daughters. Men pass on sex-linked genes only to daughters, as sons receive the Y chromosome which does not carry a colourblindness gene.

sex-linked genes See *sex chromosomes* and *Morgan.*

Sutton See *Boveri.*

transgenic organism See *genetic engineering.*

variation in offspring occurs as a result of sexual reproduction and mutations. Differences or variations occur between individuals because they have different *genes*. Different *genes* occur in individuals because of fertilisation between *gametes* with different *genes*. *Gametes* become different during *meiosis* as a result of *random segregation* and *crossing over*. *Mutation* is also responsible for variation; new genes are formed. Variation between organisms is essential for *evolution* by *natural selection*. See *Part A Evolution, natural selection.*

Watson, Crick, Franklin and Wilkins developed the double helix model for *DNA* in the 1950s. Rosalind Franklin and Maurice Wilkins worked with crystals of *DNA* and obtained X-ray diffraction patterns of the molecule. James Watson and Francis Crick used these X–ray pictures to develop and build a metal model, showing the configuration of *DNA*. Only through the collaboration of all four scientists was the structure of *DNA* able to be identified.

Chapter 3

The Search for Better Health

antibodies are proteins found in the blood and lymph and are produced in the body in response to specific antigens. They are made by special white blood cells called *B lymphocytes*. The antibody combines with its specific *antigen*. This inactivates the invader and may lead to its destruction by causing it to rupture or by stimulating *phagocytosis*. Bacterial toxins may be neutralised by antibodies and then removed by phagocytes.

antibiotics are chemicals that inhibit the growth of *bacteria*, or destroy them (eg. penicillin).They do not affect viruses. They are substances originally obtained from fungi or bacteria but many are now produced synthetically.

antigens are substances that causes the immune system to make *antibodies*. Antigens are usually foreign particles made of molecules of proteins or complex carbohydrates. They are found on the surfaces of invading *microorganisms* as well as *transplanted organs* or tissues. *Toxins* made by microorganisms also act as antigens.

B-lymphocytes or B-cells are a type of white blood cell formed and matured in the bone marrow and released into the blood and lymph. B-cells respond to invading *antigens* by developing into *plasma cells* which produce *antibodies*. The short-lived antibodies combine with specific antigens. This destroys or inactivates the antigens or stimulates *phagocytosis*. Some of the B-cells form memory cells which are involved in long-term immunity. The *immune response* involving B-cells is known as the antibody-mediated immune response. Compare with T-lymphocytes. See *lymphocytes*.

bacteria are microscopic, single-celled organisms of length 2–5 micrometres. Some cause disease, while others are advantageous to other organisms. They are procaryotic cells and have no nuclear membrane. Some have a slime capsule and/or flagella.

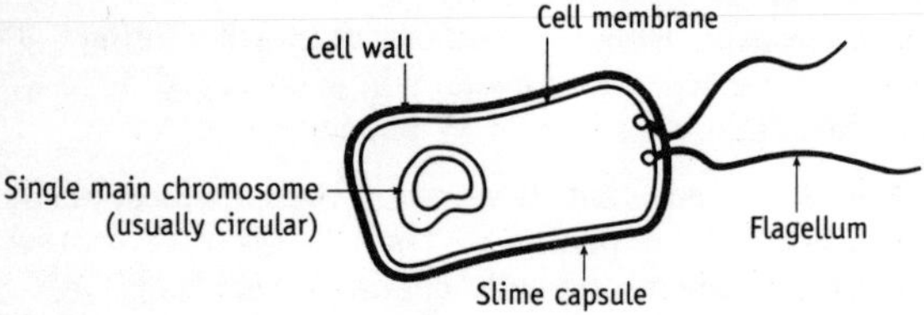

barriers prevent the entry of *pathogens* into the body. They form the body`s *first line of defence* against disease. Barriers include:

- skin which has an outer hardened layer of keratin and is waterproof. Sweat and oil glands and skin-bacteria produce antibacterial and antifungal chemicals;
- mucous membranes which line the intestines as well as the respiratory, urinary and reproductive tracts. They make mucus which traps foreign particles;

- cilia which are microscopic, hair-like structures on the cells lining the respiratory tract. Cilia beat and move mucus and foreign particles towards the throat where they are usually swallowed;
- chemicals produced by oil glands and sweat glands in the skin, as well as acid in the stomach and enzymes in the gut, which destroy *pathogens*;
- secretions such as tears, saliva and those produced in the nose. They contain enzymes called lysozymes which destroy *bacteria*.

causal agent An organism that causes an *infectious disease*.

cilia See *barriers*.

control of disease See *prevention of disease*.

disease prevents the proper functioning of the body. It may be physical, affecting the organs and tissues, but it may also affect behaviour, emotions or thought processes. See *infectious disease* and *non-infectious disease*.

environmental disease may be caused by factors in the environment including pollutants such as lead or mercury (heavy metal poisoning) or asbestos (asbestosis); stressful conditions such as noise or overcrowding (hypertension); and radiation (cancer).

epidemiology is the study of disease throughout a community. It involves the collection, documentation, and analysis of data. These studies attempt to find patterns and relationships in order to find the cause of a disease. For instance, people with a particular disease have something in common which may cause or contribute to it (eg. a very high proportion of people with lung cancer are smokers).

Patterns may be seen in the distribution of the disease, eg. *malaria* is found in tropical areas because that is where the malaria mosquito (the carrier of the disease) lives and survives.

Patterns are seen in lifestyles and occupations of diseased people, eg. skin cancer commonly occurs in people exposed to the sun, and lung diseases are found in miners (silicosis) or workers exposed to asbestos (asbestosis).

first line of defence The body prevents the entry of *pathogens* with *barriers* such as the skin and internal membranes.

fungus An organisim generally composed of thread-like hyphae and fruiting bodies producing spores.

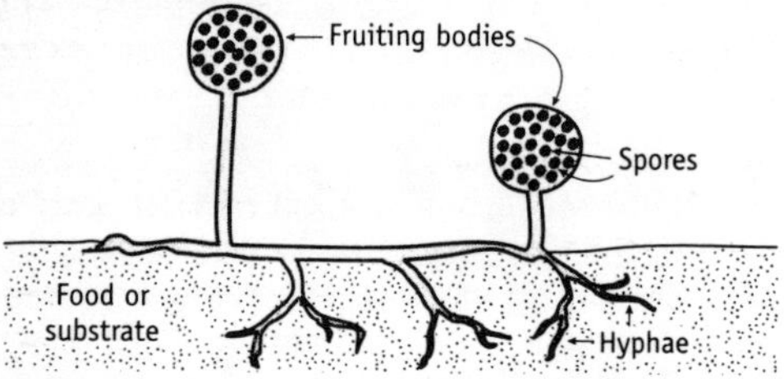

When conditions are favourable (ie. suitable temperature, food and moisture) the spores germinate to produce new hyphae that penetrate food (which may be living tissue if the fungus is a *parasite* or *pathogen*). Many fungi are useful (eg. yeast and mushrooms but many cause diseases such as tinea in animals, and rusts and smuts in plants.

health is the physical, mental and social well-being of an organism. Genes will influence health; they determine how well the *immune system* works and how resistant an individual is to disease.

immune response The production of *phagocytes* and *antibodies* when the body is invaded by *antigens*. See *third line of defence.*

immune system This includes special cells, chemicals and organs involved in the protection of the body against invading *pathogens*. See third line of *defence, and immune response.*

immunisation is the procedure used to develop an *immunity* in people by taking or injecting a *vaccine* (active *immunity*) or a *serum* (passive *immunity*). *Immunisation* programs have been successful in controlling diseases such as smallpox, diphtheria and poliomyelitis.

immunity is the ability to resist infection or to recover from it. Humans are born with *barriers*, to prevent the entry of *pathogens*. They also have *phagocytes* which attack any *pathogens* that do enter the body. These provide people with a natural resistance, sometimes referred to as natural *immunity*.

Acquired *immunity* involves *antibodies* and targets specific antigens.

Acquired *immunity* may be natural or artificial. Naturally acquired *immunity* occurs when a person is exposed to *pathogens* and their *antigens* and the body produces *antibodies* to fight them. The memory cells stay in the body and are on standby for future attacks by the same *pathogens*. The person has built up an *immunity* to this particular disease. Artificially acquired *immunity* occurs when a person is made immune by artificial means. It is done by *immunisation* using a *vaccine* or a *serum*.

Active *immunity* occurs when the *vaccine* causes the person to make *antibodies*.

Passive *immunity* occurs when *antibodies* made outside the body are introduced into the body in the form of a *serum*.

infection occurs when a pathogen enters a host.

inflammation response occurs if *pathogens* get past the *barriers* of the body and infect deeper tissues. In the infected area:

- blood vessels dilate to allow the passage of more blood;
- blood delivers *phagocytes* and *antibodies*;
- blood vessel (capillary) walls become more permeable, to increase the passage of *phagocytes* and *antibodies* into infected tissue.

As a reult of these activities the tissues become red, hot, swollen and painful.

infectious disease is caused by an *infective agent* such as a *virus, bacterium, fungus, protozoon*, or *prion*. It can be transmitted or spread to other organisms. Cholera is an example of an infectious disease. It is caused by a comma shaped bacterium called *Vibrio cholerae*, transmitted by water or food contaminated by sewage. The *bacteria* produce a toxin and enzymes which attack the intestine lining. The host responds by producing *antibodies*. Symptoms are severe bowel infection, diarrhoea, dehydration and salt loss. Infection can lead to death. It is treated by replacing fluids and salt and taking antibiotics such as tetracycline. It is prevented by cleanliness with food, and drinking only treated water, as well as by hygienic disposal or treatment of sewage and by vaccination.

infective agent An agent that invades other organisms and causes *infectious disease.*

inherited disease is non-infectious and is caused by a gene or chromosome abnormality inherited from parents, eg. haemophilia, Down syndrome, and cystic fibrosis. Gene abnormalities occur when the gene for a particular characteristic has mutated and the normal gene is replaced by an abnormal gene. Chromosome abnormalities occur during cell division (meiosis) producing cells with the incorrect number of chromosomes or with altered chromosomes. See *Chapter 2, B. Heredity and DNA, mutation.*

Koch, Robert In the mid-19th century Robert Koch researched anthrax which is caused by *bacteria* called *Bacillus anthracis*. He developed a set of procedures which made it possible to decide if a particular *microorganism* is causing a particular disease. These procedures are known as *Koch's postulates*.

Koch`s postulates are used to identify an organism as the cause of a *disease*.

1 The same *microorganism* must be present in all organisms with the *disease*.
2 The *microorganism* must be isolated, identified and cultured (grown).
3 When a healthy organism is inoculated with this cultured microbe, it must show the same disease symptoms.

4 *Microorganisms* isolated from this second host must be the same as the original, isolated *microorganisms*.

life cycle See *malaria*.

lymph fluid/vessels/nodes See *lymphatic system*.

lymphatic system
This is a series of lymph glands or nodes and one-way ducts, called lymph vessels, which carry lymph fluid. Tissue fluid from between cells, which contains *macrophages* and foreign bodies including *bacteria*, passes into the *lymph vessels*. The vessels carry this fluid, now called *lymph fluid*, to the nodes which filter out the foreign bodies. The filtered *lymph fluid* then drains into a vein at the base of the neck.

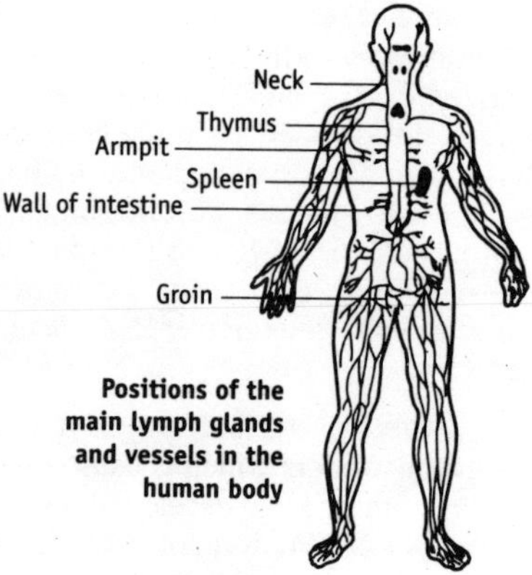

Positions of the main lymph glands and vessels in the human body

lymphocyte One type of white blood cell. Lymphocytes are produced in the bone marrow. Some mature there to form *B- lymphocytes*. Others mature in the thymus gland to form *T- lymphocytes*. B- and T- lymphocytes work together to fight *pathogens* using *antibodies* and *macrophages*. This is called the *immune response*.

Macfarlane Burnet Sir Frank Macfarlane Burnet was a great Australian medical researcher in the mid-20th century. He was interested in *infectious diseases* and how animals were protected from them. He was renowned for his research on *viruses* and immunology, which led to the development of *vaccines*. In 1955 Macfarlane Burnet proposed the clonal selection theory which provides an understanding of how the *immune system* works, how the *B-cells* respond to specific antigens, and how the body recognises its own tissues.

macrophages are a type of white blood cells which carry out *phagocytosis*. They penetrate body tissues and quickly move to sites of infection or injury. They collect damaged or worn out cells and foreign bodies, such as invading *bacteria* and their *toxins*, and carry them to the lymph vessels.

malaria is a disease of the tropics affecting birds, monkeys and humans. It produces fever, coma and anaemia. A protozoon, belonging to the genus *Plasmodium*, causes the infection. Ronald Ross in 1897 discovered that mosquitoes transmit malaria. Giovanni Grassi identified the mosquito called *Anopheles* as the carrier or vector. In humans *Plasmodium* reproduces in the liver and blood cells, destroying tissue and causing sickness.

Its life cycle is:

1 Mosquito sucks blood containing male and female forms of *Plasmodium*, called gametocytes.
2 In the mosquito stomach the gametocytes form gametes.
3 Fertilisation occurs and the zygote burrows into the stomach wall to form a cyst.
4 Cyst cells divide to form spindle-shaped cells called sporozoites.

5 Sporozoites pass into the mosquito saliva and then into human blood.
6 Sporozoites pass to the human liver. They then infect both liver and blood cells.
7 Sporozoites develop into merozoites which multiply asexually and infect more liver and blood cells.
8 Some merozoites in the blood form gametocytes.
9 Gametocytes are sucked up by mosquitoes.

Methods of control include:
- spraying mosquitoes with insecticides;
- destroying the water habitats of mosquito larvae and pupae by draining swamps;
- covering water surfaces with oil so that mosquito larvae and pupae cannot breathe;
- use of anti-malarial drugs such as quinine and chloroquine;
- use of protective clothing and nets.

microbe See *microorganisms.*

micrometre or micron (μm) is a millionth of a metre; thousandth of a millimetre, 10^{-6}m, 10^{-3}mm, (1000 μm = 1 mm)

microorganisms (microbes) are living things which are microscopic.

mucous membranes See *barriers.*

non-infectious disease includes any disease not caused by an *infective agent*. It is the result of an imbalance in nutrition (eg. obesity), heredity (eg. haemophilia), and factors in the environment such as pollutants (eg. lead poisoning). It cannot be transmitted to other organisms.

See *inherited disease, nutritional disease, environmental disease.*

nutritional disease occurs if the diet does not provide the requirements for growth and development and the correct and efficient functioning of the body. For instance, vitamin and mineral deficiencies cause diseases such as scurvy (vitamin C deficiency), and rickets (calcium deficiency).

organ transplants See *transplanting of organs and tissues.*

parasite An organism that lives in (endoparasite, eg. tapeworm) or on (ectoparasite, eg. tick) the body of another organism and feeds from it.

Pasteur, Louis In the 19th century Louis Pasteur's experimentation showed that *microorganisms* cause decay. These *microorganisms* are in the air and do not develop spontaneously from food substances. Pasteur's classic experiment follows:

Flasks contain nutrient broth which has been boiled to kill microorganisms.

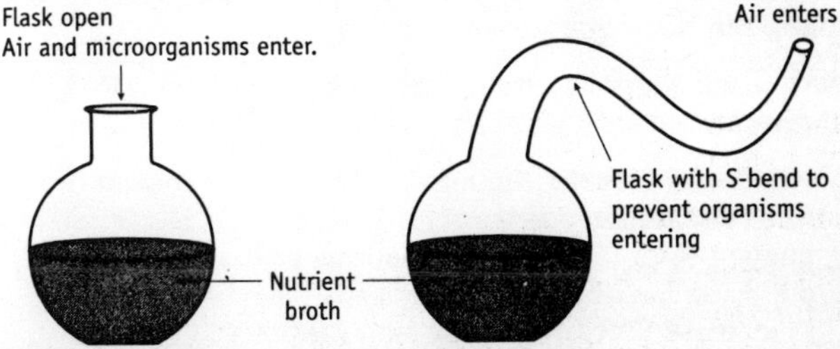

Results: Microbes grow. No microbes grow.

Conclusion: New life in the broth has come from microbes in the air.

The work of Louis Pasteur and Robert Koch proved that *microorganisms* cause disease and that they come from other *microorganisms*.

pathogen An organism which causes *disease* (eg. *virus, bacterium, protozoon, fungus*). They cause disease when conditions are suitable for them to multiply and spread. Uncleanliness and poor hygiene increase the chances of infection by pathogens.

phagocytes (eg. *macrophages*) are certain white blood cells that can leave the blood vessels and enter the surrounding tissues. They engulf the invading *pathogens* or other particles (such as damaged cells) and may destroy them. This process is called *phagocytosis*. During the attack some phagocytes are killed. Together with the *pathogens* they form pus.

phagocytosis occurs when certain white blood cells, called *phagocytes*, surround a foreign particle such as a *bacterium*. The *bacterium* is engulfed in a vacuole. The *phagocyte* produces enzymes which are released into the vacuole and digest the *bacterium*.

plasma cells develop from *B-lymphocytes* and produce *antibodies*.

prevention of disease Strategies (methods) to prevent or control disease include:

- public health programs that endeavour to educate the public on health issues. Campaigns have been organised to increase fitness, decrease skin cancer, and limit the spread of AIDS;

- immunisation programs set up to control diseases such as rubella and poliomyelitis, health screening to help detect disease in its early stages (eg. promoting Pap smears for cervical cancer, and mammograms for breast cancer);
- use of pesticides which are chemicals used to control pests that may cause disease in plants and animals. For instance, flies may carry bacteria and cause disease by contaminating food. Pesticides include insecticides, fungicides and weedkillers;
- biological control which is a method of combating pests and disease by introducing a predator of the pest. For instance, a farmer who has an infestation of scale insects may introduce ladybird beetles to prey on them;
- genetic engineering to increase resistance to disease and pests. For instance, crop plants may be given an extra gene to help them resist attack by certain viruses. Animal stock may be given genes to make them resistant to attack by pests such as blowflies and lice;
- hygiene which involves cleaning cooking and eating utensils, hands and body;
- sanitation systems to carry dirty water and sewage to treatment plants;
- *quarantine* stations to keep suspect animals, plants and people in isolation until cleared.

prion An altered protein which causes disease such as BSE (bovine spongiform encephalopathy or mad cow disease) or CJD (Creutzfeldt–Jacob disease). These diseases result in brain deterioration.

protozoa are single-celled animals which are amoeboid or have cilia or flagella. They may cause diseases such as dysentery, giardia or malaria.

Trypanosomes cause sleeping sickness.

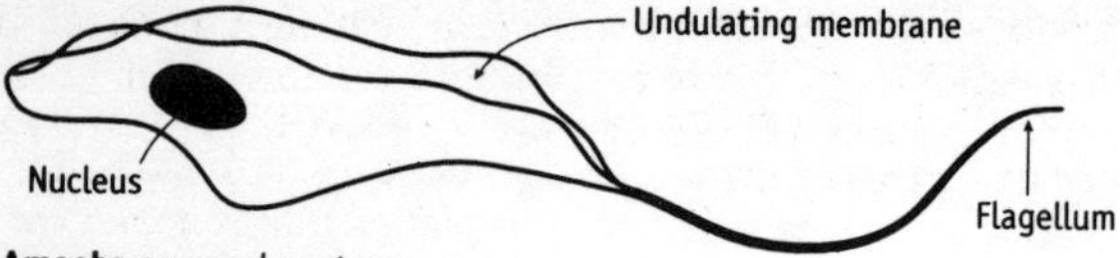

Amoeba causes dysentery.

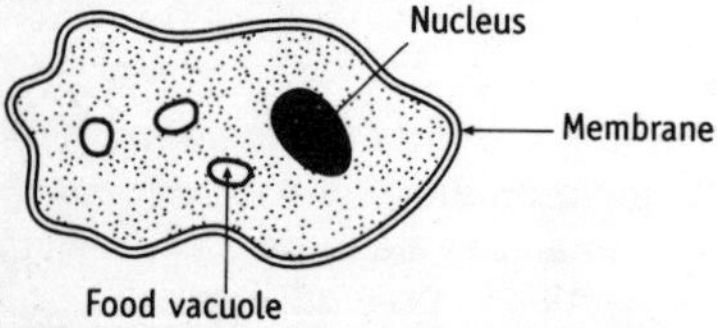

quarantine laws have proved to be successful in preventing spread of disease in Australia. All imported plants and animals are isolated for a period of time before being permitted into the community. This ensures that the incubation period for any *pathogen* they may be carrying has elapsed. Items which may be contaminated, such as agricultural equipment, are examined and cleaned and/or sprayed. Quarantine laws also prevent certain items (such as fruits) from being carried interstate, to control the spread of pests such as fruit fly.

resistance Procedures developed to increase resistance to disease may create problems, for instance:

- crops which have been genetically modified to be resistant to a pest, may cross-pollinate other plants in the community, passing on the modified genes and causing their offspring also to have this resistance. This may produce 'superweeds' which are not affected by weedkillers;

- continued use of specific *antibiotics* (eg. penicillin) has produced new strains of *bacteria* which are unaffected by these antibiotics. Many pest insects are now resistant to pesticides such as DDT as a result of continued use. See *Chapter 2, Blueprint of Life—A. Evolution, natural selection.*

Ross, Ronald identified the mosquito as the *vector* for *malaria* in 1897. He won the Nobel Prize for medicine in 1902 for his work on *malaria.*

second line of defence or *phagocytosis.* This occurs if *pathogens* or foreign substances get past the *barriers.* They are engulfed by *phagocytes* (eg. *macrophages*) which may destroy them and carry them to the *lymph system* for disposal. The second line of defence involves the *inflammation response.*

serum A liquid containing *antibodies*. It is usually prepared by injecting the disease organism or *toxin* into an animal. This stimulates the animal's immune system to produce *antibodies* which are then extracted from the blood, made into a *serum* and used for *immunisation.*

T-lymphocytes or T-cells are a type of white blood cell produced by stem cells in the bone marrow. They mature and are stored in the thymus (a lymphatic organ in the chest). *Antigens* stimulate the *T-cells* so that they divide and develop into:

- killer *T-cells,* which inactivate or destroy the *pathogen* or *toxin* and increase *macrophage* activity;
- helper *T-cells,* which activate the killer *T-cells* and *B-cells* to make *antibodies;*
- memory *T-cells* involved in *immunity;*

- suppessor *T-cells* which deactivate *B-* and *T-cells* when the infection is over.

The *immune response* involving *T-cells* is known as the cell-mediated immune response. Compare with *B-lymphocytes*. See *lymphocyte*.

third line of defence or **immune response** This occurs when the body defends itself using special *lymphocytes* which are called *B- and T-cells*.

toxin A poisonous substance produced by living things, particularly *bacteria* and other *microorganisms*.

transmission Diseases are transmitted or spread by:
- direct contact by touching infected persons;
- indirect contact via the air or contaminated objects, water or food;
- *vectors* such as mosquitoes.

Spread of disease may be reduced by promoting cleanliness, hygienic preparation of food and treatment of water (eg. chlorination).

transplanting of organs and tissues An organ which has been transferred from one person to another behaves as an *antigen* as it is foreign matter. The recipient will produce *antibodies* to 'fight' the new tissue, causing it to be rejected. To reduce the risk of rejection, the tissue of both persons must be closely matched. The recipient takes immunosuppressive drugs to suppress the *immune system*. Unfortunately these drugs also make the person prone to attack by disease organisms.

vaccination is the injection or swallowing of a substance (*vaccine*) which stimulates the *immune system* to make *antibodies*. It provides an artificially acquired *immunity.*

vaccine A chemical, injected or swallowed, to provide the body with *immunity* to a disease. The vaccine stimulates the body to make *antibodies*. There are 3 types of vaccine:

- killed *bacteria* or *viruses* (eg. cholera vaccine);
- live weakened *pathogens* (eg. rubella vaccine);
- modified bacterial *toxin* (eg. tetanus or diphtheria vaccines).

vector An organism which carries a *pathogen* from one living organism to another. For instance, rat fleas (vector) carry the *bacteria* causing bubonic plague from one human to another; the *Anopheles* mosquito (vector) carries protozoa which cause *malaria.*

virus A non-cellular organism of size 0.01–0.3 micrometres. It is composed of a protein coat surrounding DNA or RNA. It reproduces only when inside cells. Viruses are all parasitic on their host cells, causing diseases such as influenza, tobacco mosaic virus and herpes. They cannot be controlled with antibiotics.

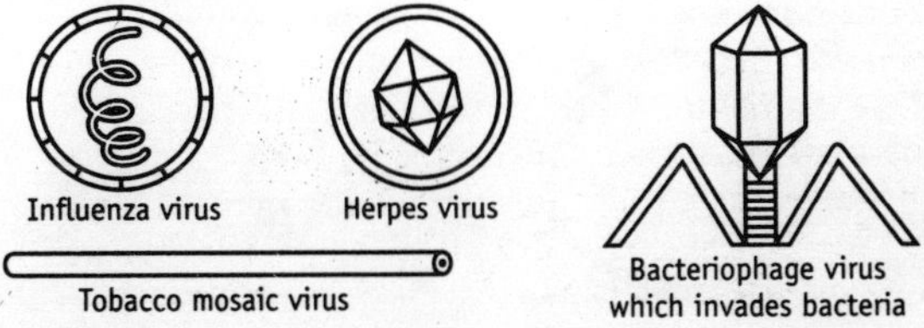

CHAPTER 4

Communication

accommodation is the method used by the eye to obtain a sharp focus by changing the thickness of the lens. It occurs when light from objects at different distances is focused on the retina. When the eye views an object in the distance, the light rays are parallel and come to focus on the *retina* with a thin lens. To view this same object clearly at a close distance, the lens increases its focusing power by becoming thicker. The ciliary muscles, at the front of the *eye*, tighten to increase the curvature of the lens (it becomes thicker). Maximum accommodation occurs when viewing very close objects.

Accommodation

(a) Distant object
- ciliary muscles relaxed
- lens thin

∴ less refraction

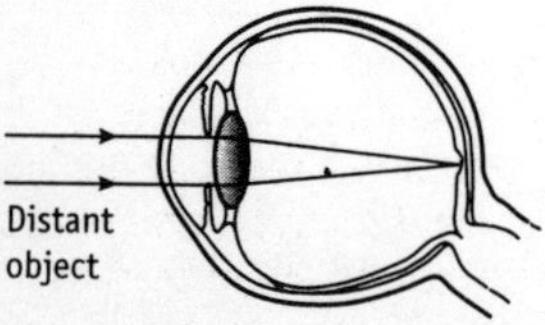

(b) Close object (accommodation)
- ciliary muscles contract
- lens thick

∴ more refraction

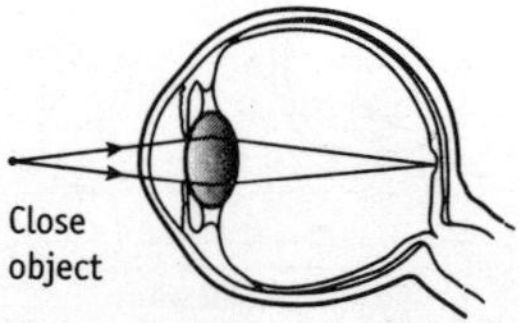

See *convex lens.*

action potential occurs when a *nerve* is stimulated. It is caused by the passage of ions through the neurone membrane, causing changes in charge. See *nerve impulse.*

acuity See *visual acuity.*

brain See figure.

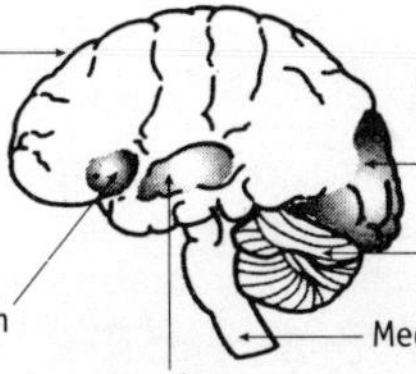

cataract A clouding of the lens in the *eye* or the capsule supporting the lens. This interferes with *light* reaching the *retina* and causes blurry vision or blindness. *Cataracts* are treated by removal of the *lens*. The *lens* is broken up by ultrasound vibrations or laser beams. The broken pieces are then sucked into a tube-like instrument which is inserted in the eye by a small incision in the cornea or they are absorbed by the body. A plastic lens is then inserted into the eye.

cochlea See *ear.*

cochlea implants are used in people who have loss of hearing because of damage to the cilia (hairs) in the cochlea. The implant is a device that bypasses the cilia and electrically stimulates the optic nerve directly. It works best for people who already understand speech. Hearing aids amplify sound, but are ineffective if cilia are damaged, as the sound waves still cannot stimulate the *nerve*.

colourblindness is usually caused by a lack of one or more pigments in the cones. See *photoreceptor cells.* It is usually a result of an inherited gene. People with normal colour vision have three light-sensitive pigments. If the 'red' or 'green' pigment is missing, blue-green colourblindness occurs. If the 'blue' pigment is missing, then blue-yellow colourblindness occurs. See *Chapter 2, Blueprint of Life— B, Heredity and DNA, sex chromosomes.*

colour vision Research involving behavioural testing, examination of eye pigments and behaviour in nature (eg. as mating rituals and warning signals using colour) indicates that a number of animals have colour vision. Colour vision is present among birds, fish, cats, dogs, monkeys and insects such as bees which can also detect UV light. Nocturnal animals have very few cones and so cannot detect colour. See *photoreceptor cells, electromagnetic spectrum.*

communication is the transfer of information between organisms. It increases the organisms' chances of survival by helping them to defend themselves and to find food, shelter, and mates. It is most advanced in social animals. The *senses* are used to detect *communication* signals. See *senses.*

cones See *photoreceptor cells.*

convex lens A lens that is thick at the centre. The lens in the eye is biconvex. A biconvex lens causes a parallel beam of light to converge at a point called the focus. The distance from the centre of the lens to the focus is the focal length. As the lens becomes thicker the focal length decreases. An eye focusing on a close object has a thick lens (increased curvature) with a small focal length. When the eye focuses on distant objects, the lens is thin (decreased curvature) and has a long focal length.

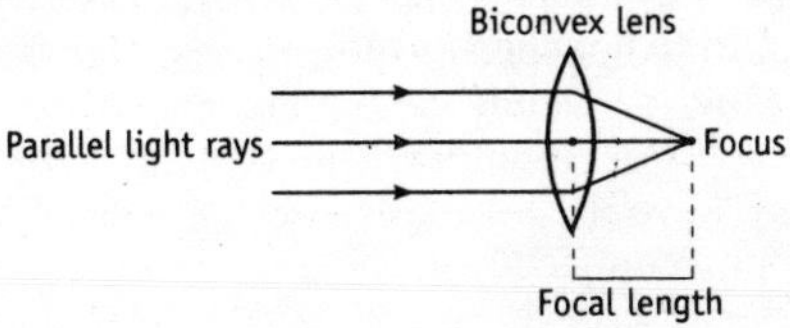

depth perception is provided by binocular or stereoscopic vision which occurs when the eyes are in the front of the head. Each eye has a slightly different image of the same object. This occurs because of the distance between the eyes and the angle at which the object is viewed by each eye.

Depth perception is also provided by cues such as that objects in the distance are smaller or may be blocked from view by a closer object.

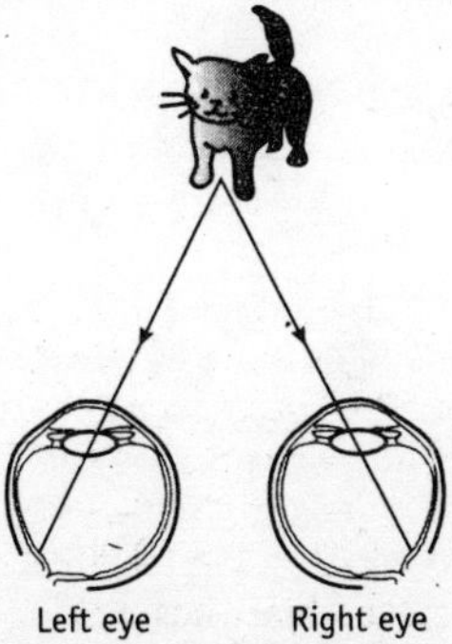

detection of vibrations In fish, vibrations are detected by pressure-sensitive receptors in the lateral line along the body. Fish also have ears which help with the orientation of the body and in many species they are used for *hearing*. There is no outer or middle ear; sound waves are absorbed by the body and the vibrations pass directly to the inner ear. Some fish have the inner ear attached to the swim-bladder by bony connections; this improves their sense of hearing. Certain insects have organs that detect vibrations (eg. anal cerci in cockroaches). Insects that make sounds have sense organs for hearing (eg. a stretched membrane which vibrates and stimulates neurones). Insect hearing organs may be found on the abdomen (grasshopper), the legs (ants), thorax (moths), and antennae (mosquito). Hearing is well developed in mammals. See *ear, hearing*.

ear See figure.

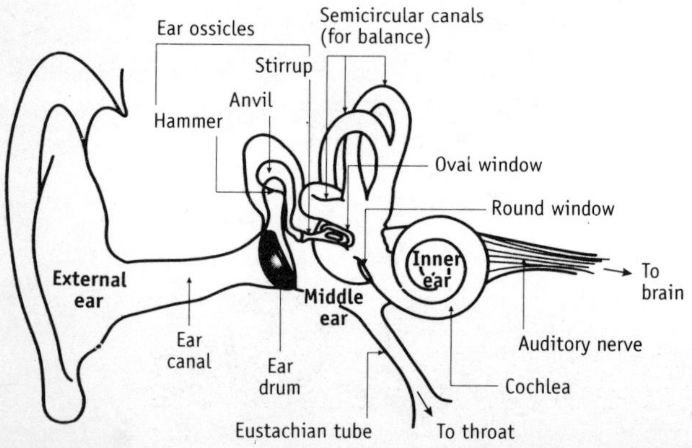

The pinna, or ear flap, directs sound waves into the ear canal. These waves cause vibrations in the tympanic membrane (ear drum) and then the ossicles vibrate. Ossicles consist of three bones called malleus, incus and stapes (hammer, anvil, stirrup). They transmit vibrations to the oval window, a membrane joining the stapes to the cochlea. Vibrations in the oval window cause fluid and membranes in the cochlea to pulsate and this causes movement in sensory hairs in the *organ of Corti.* The hairs bend and stimulate *neurones*, causing electrical impulses to travel along the auditory nerve to the *brain*. The sound vibrations in the cochlea fluid are dissipated at the round window (membrane) at the end of the cochlea tube.

effector A body structure that responds to a *stimulus*. In humans, muscles and glands are effector organs.

electromagnetic radiation A large group of radiation waves that all travel at the same speed (300 million metres/s) but have different frequencies and wavelengths. The rods and cones in the human eye are sensitive to only a small portion of the spectrum (ie. visible light).

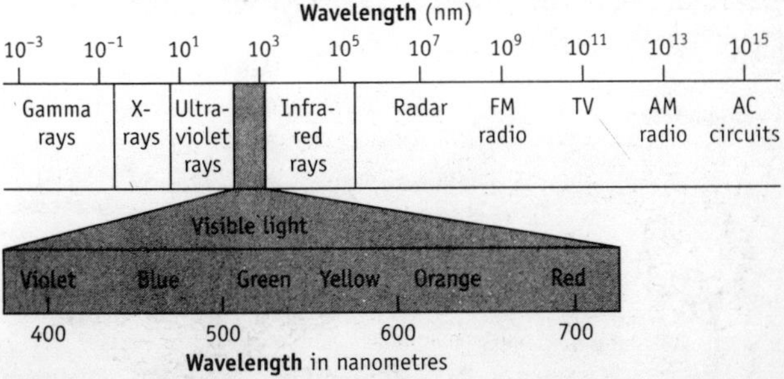

Wavelength is the distance between two wave crests. Wavelengths of visible light range between 400 nm (blue light) and 700 nm (red light). Humans are most sensitive to green light (560 nm). (nm = nanometre = 10^{-9}m) (1 000 000 000 nm = 1 m). See *colour vision.*

Eustachian tube A tube that links the middle *ear* with the throat. This enables air pressure to be equalised on both sides of the eardrum so that it will vibrate efficiently.

eye An eye is a group of receptors which are sensitive to *light* and on which an image is formed. Very simple eyes consist of a cup containing photosensitive cells connected to *neurones*. Animals with these eyes (eg. flatworms, marine molluscs) see light and shade. Most animals have eyes with focusing lenses which produce a sharp image. There are two types of lens eye; the single lens eye (eg. *eye in humans*) and the multiple lens eye (compound eye) seen in insects. The insect eye is made up of many units called ommatidia. Each ommatidium has a cornea, crystalline cone, a rhabdom and about eight light-sensitive retinal cells. The cornea and crystalline cone focus incoming light onto the rhabdom which passes it to retinal cells. Pigment cells prevent leakage of light.

Simple eye

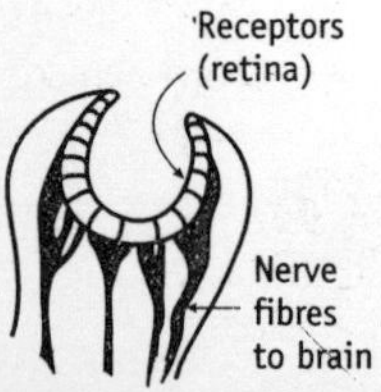

Multiple lens eye

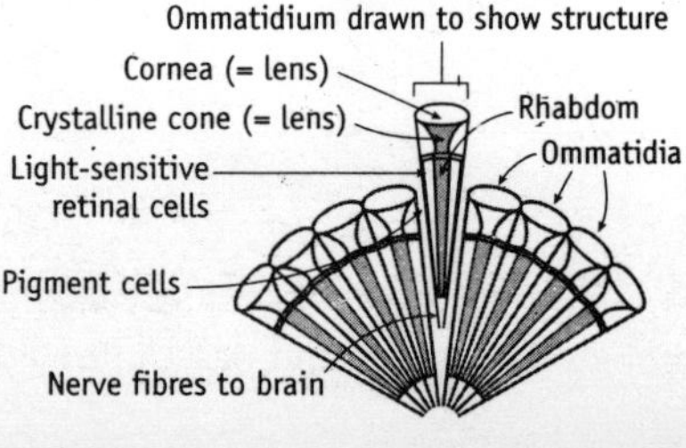

eye in humans

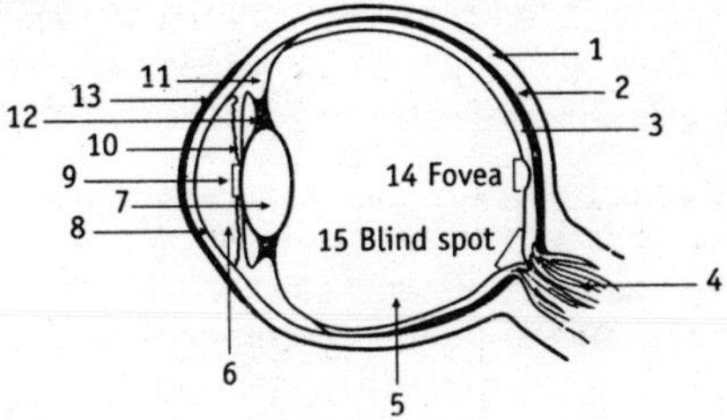

Label	Structure	Function
1	Sclera	protective layer
2	Choroid	prevents reflection
3	Retina	holds light-sensitive receptors (rods, cones)
4	Optic nerve	carries impulses to brain
5	Vitreous humour	} maintains eyeball shape and refracts light
6	Aqueous humour	
7	Lens	focuses light on retina
8	Cornea	allows entry of light and focus
9	Pupil	controls amount of light entering eye
10	Iris	changes size of pupil
11	Ciliary muscle	changes lens shape
12	Ligament	connects ciliary muscle to lens
13	Conjunctiva	protects cornea
14	Fovea	produces best image (many cones)
15	Blind spot	produces no image (no retina)

The visual process begins when *light* enters the eye through the cornea, and passes through the aqueous humour, pupil, lens and vitreous humour. *Light* is focused on the *retina* by the cornea and the lens. See *convex lens, accommodation.*

focal length See *convex lens.*

frequency of sound Humans can detect sound frequencies (pitch) between 20 and 20 000 hertz (Hz) but they are most sensitive to frequencies between 1000 and 10 000 Hz. Some animals are sensitive to frequencies outside this range. The dolphin is sensitive to sounds beyween 100 and 200 000 Hz but is most sensitive to 10 000 – 100 000 Hz. Dogs hear between 15 and 50 000 Hz, but their most sensitive range is similar to that of humans. Generally an animal's hearing range is similar to the range of sounds it produces. See *sound.*

hearing is the perception of vibrations. It provides information about the environment. An organism's ability to hear is related to its lifestyle; the frequencies it hears are usually similar to the frequencies of the sounds it makes. For instance elephants produce low frequency sounds which cannot be heard by humans, but they can be heard by mates several kilometres away. Bats have poor eyesight and so navigate by high frequency sonar; the sounds they produce are similar in frequency to the sounds they hear so that they can detect echoes. See *detection of vibrations.*

hyperopia or **longsightedness** A person is able to see distant objects clearly but is unable to see close ones. The light from near objects does not focus on the *retina*; it would focus behind the eye if it could pass through the muscular wall. Hyperopia is corrected with lenses (eg. spectacles). Compare with *myopia.*

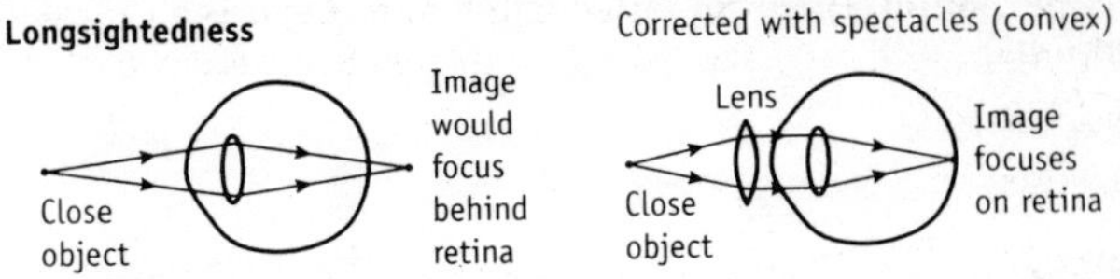

impulse See *nerve impulse.*

larynx or **voice box**. A cartilaginous chamber, at the top of the wind-pipe, containing the vocal cords. During speech, the vocal cords are stretched over the opening of the larynx. As air passes out of the lungs, the vocal cords vibrate and produce sound. Pitch is controlled by the tightening (high pitch) and relaxing (low pitch) of the cords. The larynx controls the volume and pitch of the voice, while articulation and words are produced by the teeth, tongue, palate and lips.

light enables organisms to receive information from the environment and is essential for visual *communication*. Light is a member of a large group of transverse waves called *electromagnetic radiation*. Light may be dispersed into different colours and each colour has its own wavelength.

messenger Electrochemical impulses carry messages in *nerves*.

myopia or **shortsightedness**. A person is able to see near objects clearly but not distant objects. This occurs when *light* from distant objects is focused in front of the retina. It is corrected by lenses (eg. spectacles). Compare with *hyperopia*.

Shortsightedness

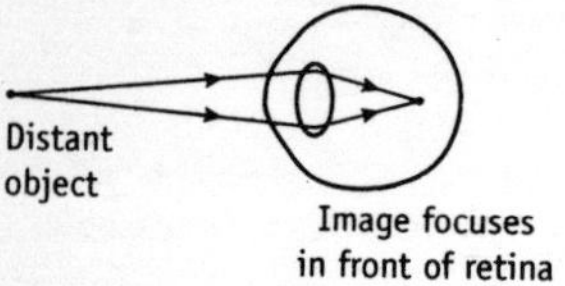

Corrected with spectacles (concave)

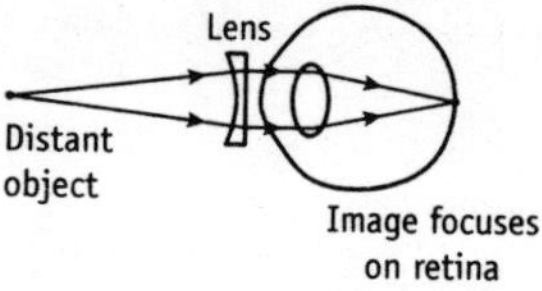

nerves transmit electrochemical messages to and from the *brain* or spinal cord. A nerve is made up of bundles of *neurone* fibres. See *nerve impulse.*

nerve impulse An electrochemical message sent along the *neurones*. When at rest, the outside of the *neurone* membrane is positively charged. This charge is caused by the presence of positive sodium ions, which have been pumped out of the neurone. The cell is said to be polarised. When the *neurone* cell is stimulated, the sodium ions move into the cell at the point of stimulation, causing a temporary positive charge (for a millisecond) in the cell. The cell is depolarised. Positive potassium ions are forced out to restore the charge to the rest state (repolarised). This excitation or impulse is called an *action potential.* If stimulation is strong enough to reach a critical point called the threshold, the *action potential* causes sodium and potassium ions in the neighbouring area to pass through the membrane in a similar manner. A chain reaction occurs so that an *action potential* moves along the neurone. The *action potential* may be shown graphically. See figure.

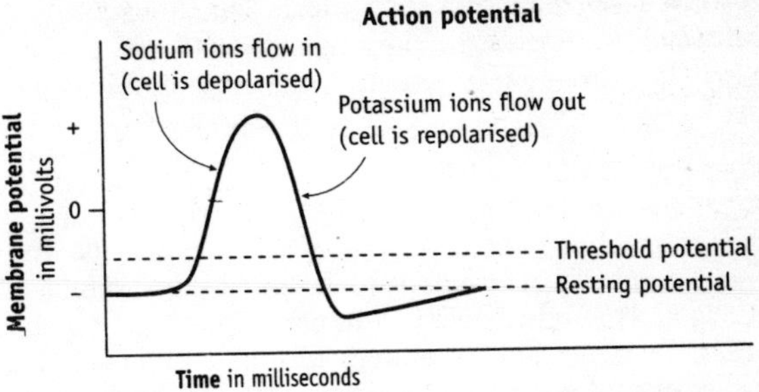

Between *neurones*, transmitter chemicals continue the impulse across the *synapse* (gap between neurones).

neurone A *nerve* cell. Each nerve contains thousands of neurones. Neurones transmit signals by electrochemical changes in their membranes. Electrical impulses pass along the *neurone* and chemicals continue the impulse between *neurones*.

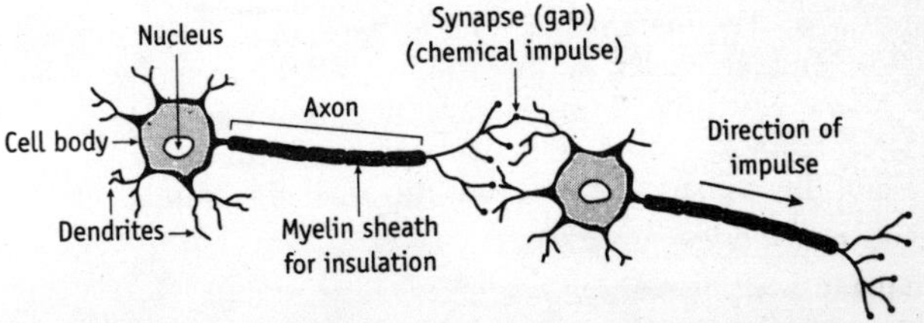

organ of Corti Found in the cochlea, it is made up of membranes and sensory hairs, or cilia, which are stimulated by vibrations caused by *sound*. Each sound frequency stimulates specific cilia. High frequency sound waves stimulate cilia at the beginning of the cochlea, near the oval window. Low frequencies stimulate at the far end (or apex) of the cochlea.

photoreceptor cells are light-sensitive *neurones* found in the *retina*. They are rods and cones and transform *light* energy into electrical energy by activation of visual pigments. The pigment in the rods is rhodopsin and is sensitive to blue-green light. The rods detect low intensity (dim) light and so are useful at night and are prominent in nocturnal animals. However, rods are not good at detecting small detail and so nocturnal animals have low *visual acuity*. Cones need more intense light to function and are most active in daytime vision. They have high acuity (provide sharp vision) and are essential for colour vision. There are three types of cones and each one is sensitive to different wavelengths of light; they are referred to as 'red', 'blue' and 'green' cones. Rods are distributed through the retina but are not found in the fovea. Cones are concentrated in the fovea and only small numbers are found in the outer areas of the *retina*. Diurnal or daytime animals tend to have more cones in the *retina*, and large eyes, so that the image falls on many *receptors*. Nocturnal animals have more rods and large lenses. Some nocturnal animals have a reflecting surface behind the retina (tapetum) that increases the amount of light reaching the *receptors*.

pigment See *photoreceptor cells*.

receptor A cell that receives stimuli from the environment and sends messages to the central nervous system. Types of receptors are:

- *photoreceptors* which are stimulated by *light* and produce the sensation of sight;
- chemoreceptors which are stimulated by chemicals in solution; they provide the sense of taste and smell;
- mechanoreceptors which respond to mechanical stimuli (such as pressure and sound) and provide the sensation of touch, pain, *hearing* and position;
- thermoreceptors which are stimulated by changes in temperature and provide the sensation of heat and cold.

reflex arc A unit of the nervous system that brings about a quick response in an organism. Consider the reflex of jerking the hand away when it touches a hot object. *Receptors* in the skin of the hand receive a *stimulus* from the hot object. Messages in the form of *nerve impulses* are sent to the spinal cord. Messages return from the spinal cord to muscles in the arm (*effector*) causing them to contract (*response*) and the hand withdraws from the hot object.

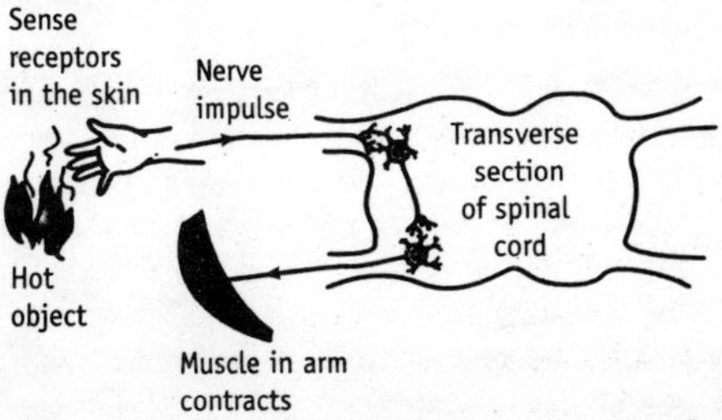

A reflex does not involve the brain.

refraction is the bending of *light* as it passes from one substance (medium) to another. When light strikes a denser medium at an angle (other than a right angle) the light slows down, causing it to bend. Light is bent towards the normal as it enters a denser substance. It bends away from the normal as it enters a less dense substance.

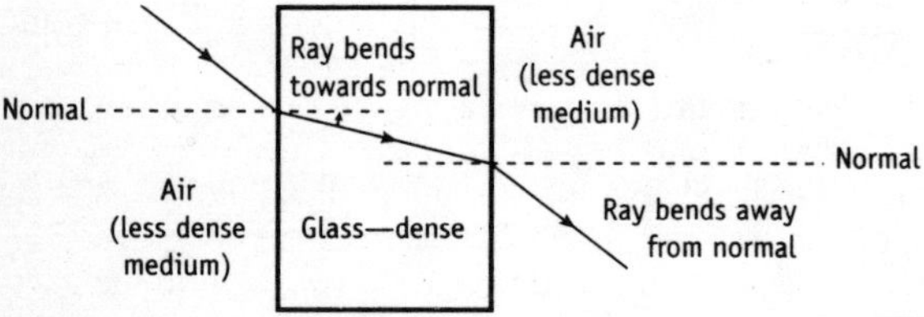

Thick slab of glass

Light passing through the cornea, the lens, and the aqueous and vitreous humours, is *refracted*, so that the light is focused on the retina.

refractive power, and hence the focusing power, of the lens in the *eye* increases as the lens curvature increases and the lens becomes thicker. When the eye views distant objects, the ciliary muscle is at rest or relaxed and the lens is thin and has a low refractive power. When the eye views very close objects, it is at maximum *accommodation*, the ciliary muscle is contracted and the lens is thick and has a high refractive power. See *convex lens*.

response is a change that is brought about as a result of a *stimulus*, eg. the stimulus of *sound* causes the response of *hearing*. See *reflex arc*.

retina This lines the eyeball and is made up of *photoreceptor cells* (rods and cones). These cells are *neurones* which are stimulated by *light* and transmit messages to the *brain*.

rhodopsin See *photoreceptor cells*.

rods See *photoreceptor cells*.

sense organs contain *receptors* which receive *stimuli* and send messages to the central nervous system (spinal cord and brain). The *brain* interprets the messages.

Sense organ	Stimulus	Sense
eye	light	sight
ear	sound	hearing
tongue	chemicals	taste
nose	chemicals	smell
skin	pressure, temperature	touch, pain heat/cold
muscles	tension	position

senses of vision, *hearing*, touch, taste and smell are all involved in *communication* and they enable organisms to become aware of their environment by means of *sense organs*. Examples of the senses as a form of *communication* are:

- *sight*—bees dance to indicate the location of food; some lizards bob their heads to indicate the species; bright colours (eg. the red stripe of a red-back spider) send warning signals to predators;
- *hearing*—speech in humans, and mating calls in birds and insects (eg. cicadas);
- *touch*—The herring gull chick pecks at a red spot on its parent's beak; the parent responds by feeding the chick. The trunk of the elephant is sensitive to touch.

- *smell*—and *taste* are interrelated. Mammals and insects produce pheromones which are involved in mating, or warn or intimidate other animals, or mark territories or trails (eg. ants). Fish can detect small changes in chemicals in the water and use this sense to recognise 'home' waters.

sonic shadow When a high frequency *sound* is located to one side of the head, the head casts a 'shadow' (caused by waves bouncing away from the head). This decreases the intensity of sound in the far ear and enables the organism to locate the sound source. Low frequency sounds have a long wavelength and generally are unaffected by the head.

sound is caused by vibrations of objects, setting up alternating high and low pressure regions in a medium. Vibrations are carried through matter, (eg. air, water, wood). Sound may be shown as a waveform using a cathode ray oscilloscope (CRO).

Sound waves travelling through air

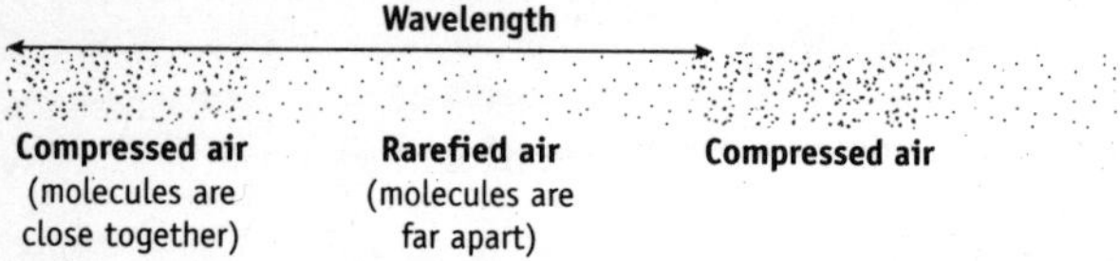

Sound waves represented by CRO

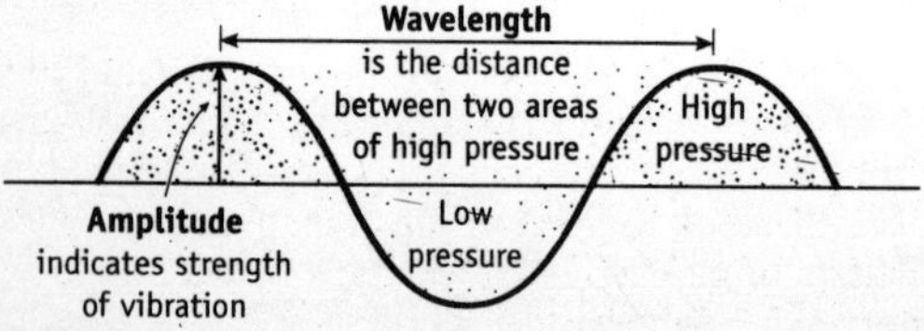

- Frequency gives the pitch of a *sound*. It is the number of times the source vibrates per second and is indicated by the number of crests that pass per second. It is measured in hertz (Hz) or cycles per second. Natural sound is usually made up of several mixed frequencies.
- Amplitude shows the intensity or volume of the *sound*. It indicates the size of the vibration from the rest position. It is measured in decibels (db).
- Wavelength is the distance between crests and indicates the distance between two areas of high pressure caused by the vibration. Humans can hear wavelengths from 20 mm to 20 m.

sound production

- *Fish*—many make sounds for shoaling, mating, warning or echolocation. Vibrations may be caused by the operculum (gill cover), vertebrae, pelvic girdle, teeth or air bladder.
- *Insects*—(eg. cicadas) produce *sound* by friction. This is caused by rubbing the wings together or rubbing legs against wings.
- *Mammals* and other land vertebrates produce *sound* by forcing air through vibrating membranes across the opening of the respiratory tract. See *larynx*.

stimulus evokes a *response* in an organism or its tissues. See *sense organs*.

synapse The gap between the axon of one *neurone* and the dendrites of the next *neurone*. The end of the axon contains sacs which produce chemicals called neurotransmitters. *Nerve impulses* reaching the end of the axon cause the neurotransmitters to pass across the *synapse* to stimulate the next *neurone*.

visual acuity is ability to see the details of an object. It can be measured in several ways; how far apart two dots have to be in order to see them as two separate dots; how large a checkerboard or vertical black and white bars need to be to be seen as a pattern. The smallest line a person can read on an eye chart indicates visual acuity. Cones have higher visual acuity than rods. Acuity increases as *light* moves closer to the fovea, ie. more cones and less rods. Acuity also increases as a person moves from dark to light, as vision changes from rods to cones. In animals the type of vision is related to its needs and its lifestyle. The compound eye in insects provides a poor granular vision as each ommatidium produces a separate and slightly different image. These eyes, however, are very sensitive to movement. Minute movements in the object will cause changes in the mosaic image. Cats see detail more poorly than humans but have a higher sensitivity to large, dim forms.

voice See *sound, larynx.*

Chapter 5
Biotechnology

agriculture is the raising of plants and animals on land, for food. Compare with *aquaculture.*

alcohol production In wine-making, yeast on the skins of the grapes acts on the sugar in the fruit, during *fermentation*. Alcohol and carbon dioxide are produced. The carbon dioxide is released in the manufacture of still wines, while it is retained in sparkling wines. If the wine is allowed to stand open to the air, bacteria will convert it to vinegar. In beer-making or brewing, brewer's yeast is added to mashed barley and water. Malt sugar in the barley is converted to alcohol and carbon dioxide. Flavour is adjusted by adding hops.

A concentration of alcohol greater than 14% will kill the yeast and *fermentation* will cease. Stronger alcohols (eg. spirits) are obtained by distillation of wine. The yeast used to produce alcoholic beverages is a species of *Saccharomyces.*

anaerobic means without air or oxygen. Microorganisms such as *yeasts* and certain bacteria respire anaerobically. This is known as *fermentation.*

antibiotics See *penicillin* and *Chapter 3, The Search for Better Health, antibiotics.*

application of biotechnology in aquaculture

- *Aquaculture* is used to grow organisms which produce useful substances. For instance: certain algae are grown as a source of chemicals needed for pharmaceuticals.
- *Aquaculture* is used for farming to provide a supply of marine animals such as abalone.

Abalone, genus *Haliotis*, is a snail-like marine mollusc. Its meat is sold as an expensive delicacy and the shells are used for ornaments and jewellery.

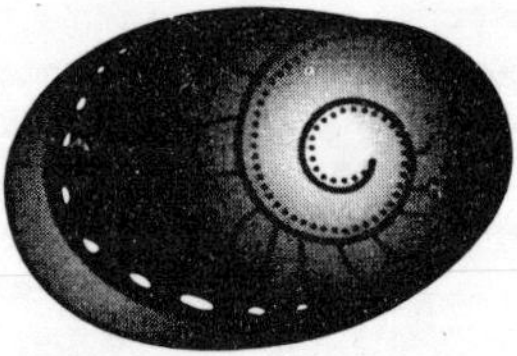

Over several decades Japan has specialised in abalone hatchery and nursery technology. The product is used to stock wild seabeds for farming. Farming of abalone can be expensive, as hatcheries need mechanisms to regulate temperature in order to control spawning. Spawning is stimulated by adding hydrogen peroxide to water or by irradiating with ultraviolet light.

Different stages of development of abalone require scrupulous hygiene, good quality ocean water and cultivated stock feed. It takes three years for abalone to reach market size. Farming provides the advantage of having abalone readily available at all times and in areas where it does not normally live. Australia earns over $130 million from abalone each year. It also helps maintain natural ecosystems as the collection of wild abalone is reduced. Disadvantages of farming include the need for careful monitoring and the expense.

application of biotechnology in medicine includes:

- tissue engineering used to *culture* host tissues such as skin for transplants;
- *nasal sprays* used for gene transfer. The sprays are used to deliver recombinant *plasmids* to cells near the mucous membranes. This method is used to deliver *recombinant vaccines*;
- synthetic hormone production (eg. insulin). See *transgenic organism*.

application of animal and plant biotechnology

- See *monoclonal antibodies.*
- See *recombinant vaccines.*
- See *genetic diversity.* Germ plasm banks are set up to maintain a source of genes, and hence diversity of organisms.

artificial selection or **selective breeding** is the selection of organisms with desired characteristics and deliberately mating them (eg. organisms which are more productive or produce a higher quality). Techniques include pedigree breeding, artificial insemination, grafting, tissue culture, in vitro fertilisation and embryo transfer. Artificial selection brings about a change in characteristics in a population. For instance, wild ancestral grasses (eg. barley, wheat) have evolved by artificial selection to cultivated cereals. In wild grasses, husks cling to the seeds to protect them and the seeds break away from the seed head easily for dispersion. The grasses have been selected to produce seeds (grain) which are free of husks, and seed heads with many seeds which cling firmly, so that they can be harvested. Wild animals (eg. boars) were ferocious. Early farmers selected and bred those tame enough to handle, and those with the desired characteristic (eg. large ones to provide more meat). See *Chapter 2, Blueprint of Life B, Heredity and DNA, selective breeding.*

aquaculture is the growing of aquatic organisms under controlled conditions. Commonly cultivated organisms are fish, molluscs, algae and crustaceans. Since 2000 BC the Chinese have raised fish by aquaculture. The Romans farmed fish and shellfish (crustaceans and molluscs). Icelanders and Aztecs harvested seaweed. There is evidence that some Australian Aborigines built canals joining swamps to farm fish. Generally, aquaculture involves food production, but, the Japanese have a long history of raising oysters for pearls.

Over 20% of Australian fish and seafood products come from aquaculture. Aquaculture is a more efficient form of food production than *agriculture.* See *application of biotechnology in aquaculture.*

biodiversity See *genetic diversity.*

biotechnology includes methods used to improve plants or animals (eg. *artificial selection*). It also includes the use of living organisms to make a product (eg. use of *yeast* to make *bread* or *alcohol)* or to modify it (eg. the use of microorganisms to convert *milk* to *cheese* or yoghurt). Currently biotechnology includes laboratory techniques such as *recombinant DNA technology* for forensic science and production of genetically modified organisms.

biotransformation technologies involve changes, at the molecular level, brought about by organisms. They have led to the production of pharmaceuticals such as cortisone (a steroid hormone) and sex hormones (eg. oestrogen) which may be produced using *fermentation* technology.

bread manufacture *Yeast* is used to make bread rise. Baker's yeast is a strain of *Saccaromyces cerevisiae.* The living *yeast* acts on starch in the flour and converts it to sugar. The *yeast* then breaks down the sugar during *fermentation* (anaerobic respiration) to produce carbon dioxide and *alcohol.* The carbon dioxide is trapped in the dough, producing air bubbles and causing the dough to rise. During baking, the *alcohol* is evaporated and the *yeast* is killed. Until the commercial production of *yeast* in the 1880s, bakers had to rely on airborne *yeast* to make bread rise. When baker's *yeast* was first produced commercially, the fungus was grown on malted grain. Later it was produced in a molasses medium.

catalyst A substance that speeds up a chemical reaction but does not take part in it (eg. *enzyme*). The concentration of the substrate (reactants) and products can be used to regulate catalyst activity. Increasing the reactants will increase the rate of the reaction, and removal of the products will increase the formation of products. For instance, *yeast fermentation* ceases when the concentration of *alcohol* reaches 14%. By removing the *alcohol* as it is produced, *fermentation* can continue.

The activity of an *enzyme* may be demonstrated using liver which contains the *enzyme* catalase. Hydrogen peroxide breaks down slowly to form water and oxygen. In the presence of catalase this occurs rapidly and oxygen gas evolves rapidly and may be tested with a glowing splint. Changes in the temperature and acidity (pH) and concentration of the hydrogen peroxide will affect the rate of the reaction.

cheese and yoghurt manufacture Cheeses were made about 2500 years ago to preserve the nutritional value of milk. In cheese making, lactic acid bacteria (species of *Lactococcus* or *Streptococcus)* are added to milk. The bacterial cultures ferment the milk sugar, lactose, to form lactic acid, increasing acidity which prevents contamination by harmful organisms. A milk-coagulating *enzyme*, rennin, is added to produce curds (solid) and whey (liquid). The curds are isolated and cooked, pressed, salted and allowed to ripen. Yoghurt-making also involves bacterial lactic acid *fermentation*. The milk–bacteria mixture is incubated at 45°C for several hours to produce acid and flavour.

citric acid is produced in *industrial fermentation* for use in the food industry for flavour and as a source of vitamin C.

culture is the growing of specific tissues or microorganisms (eg. fungi or bacteria) into colonies in or on a nutrient medium (eg. agar).

DNA is a long, twisted double-stranded (double helix) molecule in the nucleus controlling the metabolism in the cell. RNA is a shorter single-stranded molecule occurring throughout the cell. Both are made up of nucleotides (molecules containing a phosphate, sugar and nitrogen base).

DNA analysis in *forensic science* allows the matching of DNA samples left at the scene of a crime and that of the suspect. See *Chapter 2, Blueprint of Life B, Heredity and DNA*.

enzymes are proteins that make specific metabolic reactions happen. They are sensitive to temperature, pH levels and concentrations of substrate and products. Enzymes are important in biotechnology. For instance, the enzymes of bacteria are used as *restriction enzymes* to cut DNA into fragments in *recombinant DNA technology*. See *catalyst* and *Chapter 1, Maintaining a Balance*.

ethical issues concerning the use of biotechnology *Different viewpoints* occur because:

- of differences in knowledge and understanding of the processes involved;
- industrial and commercial enterprises may have a vested interest in the technology; they may make a financial gain or loss;
- consumers have access to genetically engineered pharmaceuticals, such as insulin and growth hormone, which otherwise may be very expensive or difficult to obtain;
- environmentalists show concern about how technology may affect the environment and biodiversity;
- scientists and researchers have an opportunity to contribute to areas such as better health care, agriculture and food supply.

The issues are:
Genetically modified organisms (GMO)

- The effects of long-term use of genetically modified food are not known.
- Humans are changing the course of evolution.

- Genetic modifications may be accidentally released into the environment and interfere with other organisms (eg. herbicide-resistant plants may interbreed with weeds, which will then also become resistant).
- GMO used to 'clean up' the environment may invade other ecosystems.
- GMO may be used for biological warfare.

Cloning
- Humans are producing populations of identical organisms and interfering with biodiversity and evolution.
- Selection of specific characteristics at the expense of others will remove individuality.
- The use of embryos in research may be questionable.

Gene cloning
- The use of embryos to obtain stem cells for therapeutic purposes provokes views on the rights of embryos.
- There are concerns over the rights of humans to produce transgenic organisms.
- Production of transgenic organisms may interfere with biodiversity and evolution.
- Companies funding research may have control of the new products.
- It is a new source for biological warfare.

fermentation (*anaerobic* respiration) is the process which some cells (eg. *yeasts* and bacteria) use to metabolise carbohydrates. Lactic acid or *alcohol* and carbon dioxide are formed as waste products. Microbial *fermentations* are used in industry to produce commercial *alcohol* and alcoholic beverages, as well as cheeses, yoghurt and a variety of other food products. See *alcohol production*, *cheese and yoghurt manufacture* and *bread manufacture*.

forensic science analyses DNA samples found at a crime scene and compares it with the DNA of a suspect. See *Chapter 6, Option, Genetics: The Code Broken? DNA fingerprinting.*

gene manipulation involves:

- cutting and joining DNA. See *Chapter 6, Option, Genetics: The Code Broken?, recombinant DNA*;
- monitoring the cutting and joining, which is needed to ensure that the correct genes are selected for *gene splicing* and unwanted fragments are discarded;
- transforming hosts. Recombinant *plasmids* (DNA) are introduced into bacteria which are used to produce proteins such as insulin. These bacteria may also be used as vectors to introduce the new DNA into another organism; only some bacteria will take up the *plasmid*.

gene splicing is the cutting of genes from a chromosome, using *restriction enzymes*, and inserting them into another, using *enzymes* called ligases. The first *enzyme* to cut DNA at specific sites was isolated from bacteria in 1969. *Restriction enzymes* are extracted from bacteria and purified. Each *enzyme* is very specific and has the ability to precisely cut particular DNA sequences (eg. the enzyme BamHI is extracted from a *Bacillus* species and cuts the DNA base sequence GGATCC). The cut produces an end with bases exposed; this is called the 'sticky' end. The piece of DNA to be inserted is treated with the same restriction enzyme, so complementary bases will pair. The two fragments are joined by ligase, producing a *recombinant DNA*. There are over 400 *restriction enzymes* available and this technique requires careful monitoring.

See *Chapter 6, Option, Genetics: The Code Broken?, recombinant DNA*.

genetic diversity Technology which controls the production of specific organisms (eg. cloning and genetically modified organisms) will eventually decrease diversity on Earth (ie. the number of different types of organisms becomes less). For instance, crop plants with desired characteristics will be favoured, selected and grown, while wild types, or organisms of less commercial value, will be discarded. Biodiversity is essential for balance in ecosystems and for the natural course of evolution. It is also important to maintain varieties as a gene source (germ plasm banks) for introduction into existing species (eg. a wild grass, *Triticum* species, is related to cultivated wheat and has a large source of 'new' genes which can be used to improve cultivated varieties). Procedures and strategies are being developed to ensure that countries monitor and take action to protect genetic biodiversity in nature and control storage (eg. gene banks for long-term storage of eggs, sperm and embryos).

history of biotechnology Biotechnology dates back to the earliest farmers in the Middle East about 10 000 BC. They collected wild seeds, particularly those producing grain (eg. wheat and barley) and stored them in caves. Later they scattered, cultivated and harvested these seeds and eventually dug trenches for planting them and built canals and developed systems for irrigation. They also domesticated wild animals (eg. sheep, goats and pigs) and trained others (eg. horses and donkeys) for work. Farmers became aware that hybrids (the offspring of different varieties or species) were often larger and healthier. They began to breed plants and animals with desired characteristics. This was the beginning of *artificial selection.* In the 18th and 19th centuries, labour-saving machinery was developed (eg. seed drills, harvesting and threshing machines). Microorganisms have also been used in aspects of biotechnology (eg. in the production of fermented foods, and the production of pharmaceuticals). See *history of fermentation.*

history of fermentation Many fruits, saps and nectars ferment naturally and have always been used by humans. Later they deliberately fermented products to improve flavour and to help preserve nutrition. *Fermentation* has been used since ancient times to brew beer (before 6000 BC) and make bread (about 4000 BC). The role of microorganisms in the *fermentation* process was unknown. Ancient Egyptians allowed bread dough to stand for several hours before baking to produce a light bread with better flavour. They made fermented drink from barley and other grains, and wine from grapes. The microorganisms involved were either on the raw materials (eg. *yeast* grows on grape skins) or fell into the ingredients. Large-scale production of alcohols began in the 1700s. Over the next 200 years fermentation processes expanded to include the production of organic compounds such as *lactic acid, citric acid,* glycerol and *yeast biomass.* Microorganisms are now used to produce other useful substances such as fuels (eg. methane) and pharmaceuticals (eg. antibiotics and vaccines).

impact of changes in scientific knowledge and technology The traditional use of technology has been modified as follows:

- The discovery of the role of microorganisms in the production of foods and beverages has led to the commercial culturing and use of these microorganisms. Techniques have been researched to maintain consistency in cultures, which normally show high genetic variability. Large-scale production of *alcohol* and fermented foods is now possible.

- The knowledge that heat kills microorganisms has enabled better control of *fermentation* and made it safer. For instance, contamination by unwanted microorganisms can be prevented.
- Testing and control techniques provide better quality and more consistent products.
- Microorganisms which are resistant to viral attack are being developed.
- In cheese-making, microbial *enzymes* are added to accelerate ripening, which gives a distinctive flavour. Additional microorganisms are cultured and added to cheeses to provide specific characteristics (eg. the fungus *Penicillium* produces blue-green veining).
- Genetic engineering has increased the availability of microbial products. For instance, genetically engineered microbial rennin (previously obtained from the gut of calves) allows the large-scale production of cheese.

industrial fermentation Microorganisms are cultured on a large scale to enable them to produce substances which are commercially valuable or useful in industry. These products include *lactic acid, citric acid,* glycerol, and *yeast biomass.*

insulin production See *transgenic organism.*

lactic acid is produced by an industrial *fermentation* process. It is usually produced by the *fermentation* of sugar or glucose by *lactic acid* bacteria, which are species of

Streptococcus, Lactobacillus, Lactococcus or *Leuconostoc*. Sugar is combined with water, lime (calcium carbonate), and *lactic acid* bacteria. The product formed is crude calcium lactate. Gypsum is removed, leaving crude lactic acid, which is then purified and concentrated to form *lactic acid* for commercial and industrial use. *Lactic acid* is used in food products and processes such as salads, beverages, pickled vegetables, confectionery and dairy products (eg. cheese). It is also used in cosmetics and in the production of paints and detergents and in the leather, electrical, metal, tobacco and polymer industries. Industrial production has had an impact on the food industry by improving flavour and texture as well as increasing shelf-life by inhibiting the growth of other microorganisms. It has also reduced processing time. It has provided a moisturiser for the cosmetics industry. It has also improved industrial processes by assisting with acid regulation or by providing antimicrobial activity.

ligase See *gene splicing*.

monitoring of cutting and joining DNA See *gene manipulation*.

monoclonal antibodies are antibodies cloned (copied) in the laboratory. They are pure, very specific and produced in large quantities (antibodies produced in animals are a complex mixture). The procedure to produce monoclonal antibodies involves selection and cloning of lymphocytes which produce a specific antibody.

Procedure:
(1) An antigen (foreign substance) is injected into mice.
(2) The mice produce a mixture of B- lymphocytes.

(3) B- lymphocytes are removed from the mice and combined with cancerous lymphocytes to form hybrid cells. As cancerous cells are 'immortal' and grow readily, the hybrid cells have an extended lifespan and are easy to *culture.*

(4) Hybrid lymphocytes which produce the required antibody are selected and cloned. These lymphocytes supply the required antibody in large quantities.

Monoclonal antibodies are ideal for research and diagnostic purposes. They are used for tagging particular cells, detecting and diagnosing diseases such as cancer, and tissue typing for grafts and transplants. They can also be used for treatment (eg. poisons can be attached to specific antibodies and directed against tumours). See *Chapter 3, The Search for Better Health, antibodies.*

named industrial fermentation process See *lactic acid.*

nasal spray See *application of biotechnology in medicine.*

Pasteur, Louis (French scientist, 1856) conclusively proved that the *fermentation* of sugar, to produce *alcohol*, was caused by microorganisms. He carried out experiments to show that glucose produced *alcohol* when it was exposed to air containing spores of *yeast* and other microorganisms. Sterile glucose did not produce *alcohol*. He cultured *yeast* found on freshly picked grapes and showed that it fermented grape juice. He also showed that *alcohol* was oxidised to acetic acid (vinegar) by certain bacteria. He determined that different microorganisms caused different *fermentations*.

penicillin is the first naturally occurring antibiotic to be isolated and used successfully against bacterial disease. It was discovered by Alexander Fleming in 1928. He found that *Penicillium* spores inhibited the growth of bacterial colonies on agar plates. In the early 1940s, Howard Florey and his colleagues extracted the chemical from the fungus and developed it as a medication against bacterial infection. *Strain isolation techniques* and microbial metabolism involving *fermentation* technology were important in the production of penicillin and later antibiotics.

Penicillium is a fungus which produces a chemical called *penicillin* which inhibits the growth of bacteria. The fungus probably uses it for defence against competing bacteria.

plasmid A small piece of circular DNA found in organisms such as bacteria and *yeast*. Plasmids can duplicate independently of the other chromosomes and can be transferred between bacteria. Plasmids are useful in *recombinant DNA technology*.

polymerase chain reaction (PCR) This is a procedure used in *recombinant DNA technology* to make copies of the recombinant DNA. It is known as DNA amplification. In this process DNA strands are separated. A primer (a short piece of RNA), nucleotides and DNA polymerase *enzyme* are added and incubated. See *Chapter 6, Genetics: The Code Broken? recombinant DNA*.

protein and polypeptide synthesis See *Chapter 2, Blueprint of Life B, Heredity and DNA*.

recombinant DNA technology involves:

- *gene splicing;*
- amplification (making copies) of the new DNA using a process called the *polymerase chain reaction*;

- *transgenesis* (ie. insertion of this DNA into other organisms to produce *transgenic organisms*).

See *Chapter 6, Option, Genetics: The Code Broken?*

recombinant vaccines are *vaccines* produced by *recombinant DNA technology*. They reduce side-effects and the risk of actual infection, as they contain only the antigen (the protein found on the surface of the pathogen). Traditional vaccines contain other components such as weakened pathogens.

Procedure to produce recombinant vaccines: (1) The gene which controls production of the antigen protein is identified and cut out of the chromosomes of the pathogen. (2) It is inserted into a bacterial *plasmid* and cloned. (3) The bacteria now produce the antigen, which is isolated and injected into a mammal which produces the antibody against it. (4) The antibody is isolated from the mammal's blood and purified.

Research has been carried out to develop vaccines for malaria and viral pox diseases in livestock such as chickens and sheep. See *Chapter 3, The Search for Better Health, vaccine.*

restriction enzyme See *gene splicing.*

reverse transcription A technique used to produce artificial genes. In normal transcription, RNA is made by base-pairing with DNA. In reverse transcription, RNA is the template and DNA is produced from the RNA. This requires an *enzyme* called reverse transcriptase, which is extracted from retroviruses (viruses which use their RNA as a template to produce DNA). Reverse transcription also occurs in the *polymerase chain reaction*, where a primer, which is a piece of RNA, is used to provide a starting sequence for DNA replication. See *Chapter 6, The Code Broken? transcription*.

RNA See *DNA* and *Chapter 2, Blueprint of Life B, Heredity and DNA*.

strain isolation techniques were developed in the 1940s, when *Penicillium* was fermented to produce *penicillin*. These techniques enabled useful strains of microorganisms to be separated from mixed cultures. The microorganism to be isolated was selected and streaked onto a sterile nutrient agar plate with a sterile inoculating loop. The plate was then incubated to allow the new colonies to grow. These isolated microorganisms provided pure cultures which could then be grown in large quantities and used in *industrial fermentation* processes. Strain isolation was also important in the development of *antibiotics*.

tissue engineering See *application of biotechnology in medicine*.

transgenesis is the movement of genes from one organism to another. The DNA may be injected into the cells using a micropipette or a particle gun. Genes are also transferred using bacterial or viral vectors containing *recombinant DNA*. See *nasal spray*.

transgenic organism An organism which has received genetic material from another organism and can pass this DNA on to its offspring. Insulin is used to treat diabetic patients. It is made chemically but is costly. It has been produced commercially by transgenic technology. In this process mRNA is removed from human pancreatic cells. It is used to make single-stranded DNA using *reverse transcription*. DNA polymerase is then used to replicate the DNA by complementary base-pairing, This cloned DNA (carrying human insulin-producing genes) is inserted into *plasmids* of the bacterium *Escherichia coli* by *gene splicing* or the *recombinant DNA technique.* The bacteria are *cultured* and *recombinant DNA* is cloned and produced in large quantities. These bacteria are now capable of producing human insulin, which can be isolated and purified for use. This insulin has provided problems with purification and side-effects. Genetically modified *yeast*, *Saccharomyces cerevisiae*, is now often used as an alternative to bacteria. This process is cheaper than isolating and purifying insulin from animals such as pigs and cattle. See *Chapter 6, Option, Genetics: The Code Broken? recombinant DNA*.

vaccines trigger the immune response. Genetic engineering has developed *recombinant vaccines* which reduce the risk of side-effects and actual infection. Bacteria are used to produce the vaccines which contain antigens to trigger development of antibodies. See *Chapter 3, The Search for Better Health*.

yeast is a unicellular, microscopic fungus which reproduces asexually by budding (mitosis). Under unfavourable conditions it may reproduce sexually to produce hardy spores. Yeast occurs naturally on the surfaces of fruits such as grapes. Yeast produces carbon dioxide and *alcohol* during *anaerobic* respiration and is used in *bread manufacture* and *alcohol production*. *Yeasts* are commonly used in *recombinant DNA technology*.

yeast biomass Yeast is produced in large quantities for use in baking, brewing and other *fermentation* processes. Yeast biomass is produced by a controlled aerobic *fermentation*. Pure strains of the mother culture are maintained in the laboratory, then transferred to a processing plant where they are grown in a nitrogen-enriched molasses medium, fortified with vitamins and minerals for maximum cell productivity. Many generations are produced. The mature cell mass is separated from the spent liquid to form liquid cream *yeast*. This is filtered and used to produce dry *yeast* or compressed block *yeast*.

Chapter 6

Genetics: The Code Broken?

allele See *Chapter 2, Blueprint of Life B, Heredity and DNA.*

blood groups in humans The inheritance of ABO blood groups involves the *multiple alleles*, A, B and O. Alleles A and B are codominant, while O is recessive. See *Chapter 2, Blueprint of Life B, Heredity and DNA, codominance and Mendel's experiments.*

Possible genotypes for blood groups:

Blood group	Possible genotypes
O	OO
A	AA or AO
B	BB or BO
AB	AB

Blood is also grouped by the presence or absence of a particular protein on the surface of the red blood cells. This protein is called the Rh factor or rhesus factor and is present in 85% of Australians. These people are said to be Rh positive, while those without the protein are Rh negative. An Rh– person, receiving Rh+ blood will produce antibodies against the Rh factor, as it is an antigen. The gene for Rh + is dominant (R), while Rh– is recessive (rr). If an Rh– woman and a homozygous Rh + man have a child, the foetus will be Rh + (Rr). (The mother will produce antibodies in response to the child's Rh factor.) The embryo may be damaged by an antigen–antibody reaction. See *Chapter 3, The Search for Better Health, immune response.*

chloroplast An organelle in green plant cells responsible for photosynthesis. See *Chapter 8 Option—Biochemistry.*

chromosome mapping The frequency of *crossing over* is used to map the relative positions of *genes* on chromosomes. The further apart two *linked genes* are, the more *crossing over* will occur between them. The percentage of *crossing over* that occurs between two *genes* gives an indication of their distance apart. The percentage of crossing over is determined from the offspring of a test cross (ie. crossing with a recessive individual).

Consider a genotype AaBb where genes A and B are linked.

Test cross: AaBb × aabb

Most of the individuals produced will be from gametes that show no *crossing over* between these genes, (gametes = AB and ab). They will have genotypes AaBb and aabb.

	AB	ab
ab	AaBb	aabb

Some of the offspring will be *recombinants* ; they have resulted from gametes with *crossing over*, (gametes = Ab and aB). These offspring will have genotypes Aabb and aaBb.

Recombinant gametes

	Ab	aB
ab	Aabb	aaBb

chromosomes See *Chapter 2, Blueprint of Life B, Heredity and DNA*.

The recombinants and non-recombinants can be distinguished by their different phenotypes.

$$\text{The cross-over frequency} = \frac{\text{number of recombinants}}{\text{total number of offspring}} \times 100\%.$$

If the cross-over frequency between A and B is 20%, then these two genes are 20 map units apart. Consider another gene, C, with cross-over frequency of 5% between A and C, and 15% between C and B. The positions of these genes can be shown on the chromosome map:

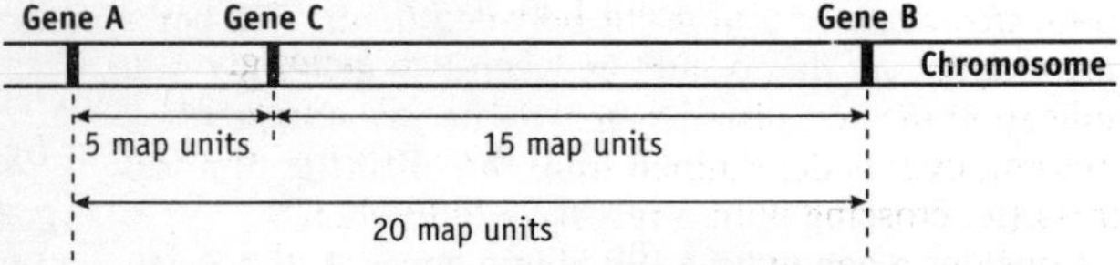

Recombinant DNA technology is also used to map chromosomes. This procedure involves cutting the DNA with *restriction enzymes*, electrophoresis to sort the fragments of DNA, and DNA sequencing, using radioactive or fluorescent probes, in the form of a fragment of mRNA or DNA. The probe will attach to its complementary DNA segment by base pairing. It is used to determine the base sequence. Chromosome maps are used to identify relationships between species. Closely related organisms will have similar base and gene sequences in the DNA. The more distantly related two organisms are, the more differences will be present.

chromosome mutation See *mutation*.

cloning is the process of making copies. Asexual reproduction occurs by mitosis, producing copies of the parent cell and so is considered an example of cloning. Likewise the growing of plants from cuttings or runners is also cloning. Cloning includes the copying of whole organisms, cells or genes.

Cloning of whole animals requires a *diploid* nucleus to be removed from a somatic (body) cell. The nucleus is transferred to an egg cell which has had its own nucleus removed. Under suitable conditions the egg will then develop into an organism identical to the donor of the nucleus. Cloning of whole organisms is faster and more predictable than *selective breeding*.

Cell cloning involves tissue culture. See *Chapter 2, Blueprint of Life B, Heredity and DNA, cloning*.

Gene cloning is the copying of DNA segments using *recombinant DNA* technology. The gene to be copied is inserted into a bacterial *plasmid* by *gene splicing*. The *plasmid* is then reintroduced into a bacterium, where it reproduces and is passed on to bacterial daughter cells. Gene cloning is used to produce medicines (eg. insulin), (see *recombinant DNA*), and transgenic species with desirable characteristics such as disease resistance. See *Chapter 2, Blueprint of Life B, Heredity and DNA, genetic engineering*.

Cloning decreases variation in the population. This may be a problem if there is an environmental change (eg. the introduction of a disease organism) as the population will be less able to adapt. Natural selection and evolution will be reduced.

Cloning may be beneficial to humans as it provides a quick reliable way to develop organisms (eg. crops) with desired characteristics.

crossing over See *linked genes.*

dihybrid cross This involves inheritance of two separate characters (eg. AAbb × aaBB or AaBb × AaBB). Consider the dihybrid cross where the two parents are hybrid or heterozygous for both genetic traits (eg. AaBb × AaBa).

- If the genes are on separate *chromosomes* (ie. they are not linked), then the gametes formed by the parents in *meiosis* will contain one of each type of gene (ie. possible gametes will be AB, Ab, aB, ab). These gametes will be produced in equal proportions. See *linked genes.*

Gametes	AB	Ab	aB	ab
AB	AABB	AABb	AaBB	AaBb
Ab	AABb	AAbb	AaBb	Aabb
aB	AaBB	AaBb	aaBB	aaBb
ab	AaBb	Aabb	aaBb	aabb

Offspring with four different phenotypes will be produced, in a 9:3:3:1 ratio. Nine offspring will have the two dominant traits or characteristics (A_B_); 3 will have one dominant and one recessive trait (A_bb); 3 will have the other dominant and recessive trait (aaB_); 1 will have both recessive traits (aabb).

- If the genes are linked (ie. on the same chromosome), they will pass into the gametes together (eg. if A and B are linked, then a and b will also be linked and the possible gametes will be AB and ab). See *linked genes.*

Two different phenotypes will appear in the offspring in a 3:1 ratio. Three will have both dominant traits (A_B_); 1 will have both recessive traits (aabb).

	AB	ab
AB	AABB	AaBb
ab	AaBb	aabb

- If the two genes are linked and *crossing over* occurs, all four gametes will be formed (ie. AB, Ab, aB, ab) but not in equal proportions. Gametes with no *crossing over* will be more common (ie. AB, ab).

diploid See *haploid.*

DNA See *Chapter 2, Blueprint of Life B, Heredity and DNA*.

DNA code (genetic code) DNA contains a code which provides instructions for the synthesis of polypeptides and proteins. This code is provided by the order of the bases along the length of the DNA molecule. It is expressed when a particular portion of the DNA or gene is active. See *gene expression* and *Chapter 2, Blueprint of Life B, Heredity and DNA, protein synthesis.*

DNA fingerprinting uses patterns in DNA base sequences. These patterns vary between individuals and each person has unique patterns. Patterns may be analysed and matched (or compared) with other DNA samples.

To obtain a fingerprint, DNA is cut into fragments and sorted by length with electrophoresis. Radioactive probes, in the form of a small segment of mRNA or DNA, are used to tag or identify the DNA fragments The probes will attach to complementary DNA segments by base-pairing. An autoradiograph is produced to show the positions of the radioactive probes and their attached DNA on X-ray film.

The spacing of the radioactive bands forms the fingerprint and can be used to make comparisons.

DNA fingerprinting is used in:

- forensic science. For instance, skin tissue or blood left at a crime scene may be analysed and compared with the tissue of suspects;
- paternity testing. Closely related people have similar patterns in DNA. The DNA of a child may be compared with that of possible fathers to establish a genetic relationship;
- pedigreeing of animals. DNA comparisons may be made to determine relationships between animals and to check pedigrees. Closely related animals will have a high degree of matching patterns.

DNA in organelles Most *DNA* is found in the nucleus. *Chloroplasts* and *mitochondria* have their own *DNA* and therefore genes. Chloroplast and mitochondrial DNA is almost always circular and is attached to the inner membrane of the *organelle*. Replication of this DNA is not in phase with *DNA replication* in the nucleus. Inheritance or organelle DNA does not follow Mendelian laws.

DNA repair Cells contain DNA repair systems. They consist of enzyme complexes which move along the DNA strands. They detect and repair irregularities such as broken bonds and incorrect base pairing. See *Chapter 2, Blueprint of Life B, Heredity and DNA*. Sometimes the repair system fails and the change or error remains in the DNA as a *mutation* .

DNA replication See *Chapter 2, Blueprint of Life B, Heredity and DNA*.

gametic cell A reproductive cell or gamete (eg. egg or sperm). It contains the *haploid* number of chromosomes.

gene See *Chapter 2, Blueprint of Life B, Heredity and DNA*. There is evidence that a specific gene may be responsible for more than one trait during the organism's lifetime.

gene cascades See *genes in embryos*.

genes in embryos During embryo development, cells become different (cell differentiation), to form tissues and organs. These changes are controlled by genes which are switched on and off at certain times and trigger development in a specific order. The products of some genes will also affect and control the expression of others. A cascade of *gene expression* occurs. This is seen in the development of the limbs of birds and mammals. First, the forelimb buds appear, then hind limb buds form. Different tissues then form in the limb buds, at specific times.

gene evolution Research indicates that genes and their base sequences have changed slowly. Organisms from different species have *gene homologues* indicating common gene ancestry. New genes have evolved by duplication of a particular gene, followed by random *mutations*. The original gene, and hence the individual, remains unimpaired. The duplicated, redundant, gene is not functional in the organism and is free to mutate without being selected against.

gene expression involves the transferring of information from the genes to the final product (ie. the protein produced in the ribosome). This process includes activation of genes, *transcription* and *translation*.

Switching genes on. All cells have a complete diploid set of genes and chromosomes. Only certain genes are active in a cell; otherwise, all cells would appear the same. Current knowledge of how genes express themselves has come from studies of bacteria. Francois Jacob and Jacques Monod formulated a model for *gene expression*. This process involves a regulator gene and an operon. An operon consists of an operator region and a group of structural genes determining structure (ie. amino acid sequence).

The operator acts as an on–off switch for the structural genes. This switch is controlled by the regulator gene. The regulator gene produces a repressor protein which binds to the operator gene and inactivates it (ie. it acts as an off switch), so that *transcription* (RNA production) is inhibited. If an inducer molecule is present, it combines with and inactivates the repressor protein. The repressor now cannot bind with the operator so it acts as an on switch and *transcription* occurs.

Operator gene switched off

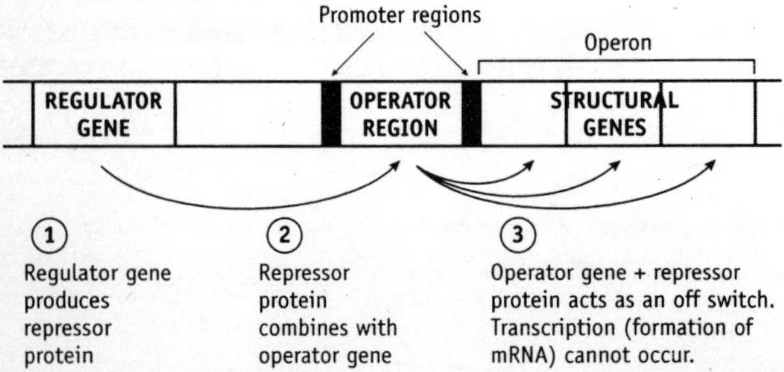

This switch mechanism involves two promoter regions located on both sides of the operator. During *transcription RNA polymerase* binds to the promoter regions.When the repressor protein binds to the operator, *RNA polymerase* cannot physically bind to the promoter and *transcription* is blocked.

gene homologues Different species have similar groups or patterns of genes that code for and control the development of the same structure. This is a *gene homologue*. It is thought that these genes in different organisms share a common gene ancestry.

gene mutation See *mutation*.

gene splicing See *recombinant DNA* and *Chapter 8, Option, Biotechnology*.

gene therapy aims to correct the effects of faulty genes. It may be used to treat genetic disorders as well as diseases such as cancer and AIDS. Several possible methods could be used. A dormant gene with a similar function may be activated to override the function of a faulty gene. Extragenetic material may be introduced into a cell to replace a faulty gene. *Recombinant DNA* technology is used to insert a gene into the patient.

Gene therapy for cancer involves using bacterial genes to produce enzymes that will convert a certain chemical so that it will destroy the tumour cells.

genome A complete set of *haploid* chromosomes and their genes. See *Human Genome Project*.

haploid Having one set of chromosomes in a cell. *Meiosis* produces *haploid* cells. These cells are usually *gametic cells* (ie. egg or sperm). The *haploid* number is given the symbol n and is half the number of chromosomes found in *somatic cells* (body cells). The number of chromosomes found in somatic cells is referred to as the diploid number, with symbol $2n$. In humans $n = 23$; $2n = 46$.

Human Genome Project An international project which has endeavoured to identify the human genes, determine their DNA sequence and map the human chromosomes. Several types of gene map have been completed and a working draft of the entire gene sequence (30 000 genes) was announced in June 2000, and analysis published in February 2001. The Project will provide a number of benefits. It will enable identification of the cause of genetic disorders. This will aid in the diagnosis, treatment and prevention of these diseases and the development of *gene therapy*. It will provide a better understanding of evolutionary relationships by enabling comparison of DNA sequences in organisms. See *Chapter 7, Option, The Human Story, DNA–DNA hybridisation.*

There are some limitations on the data obtained from the project. The *genome* provides simplified information about genes and the production of proteins. It does not include complex biochemical pathways, and information about processes involving a number of 'networked' genes is limited.

linked genes occur on the same chromosome and stay together during assortment in *meiosis*; they are usually inherited together. An organism with genes A and B linked will produce gametes AB and ab.

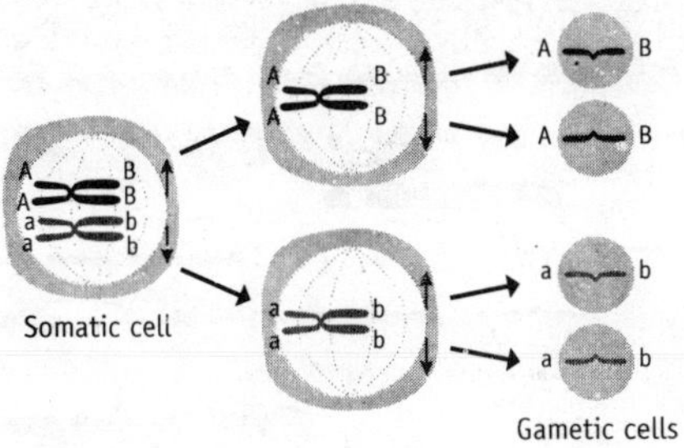

However if *crossing over* occurs, gametes AB, Ab, aB, ab will be formed.

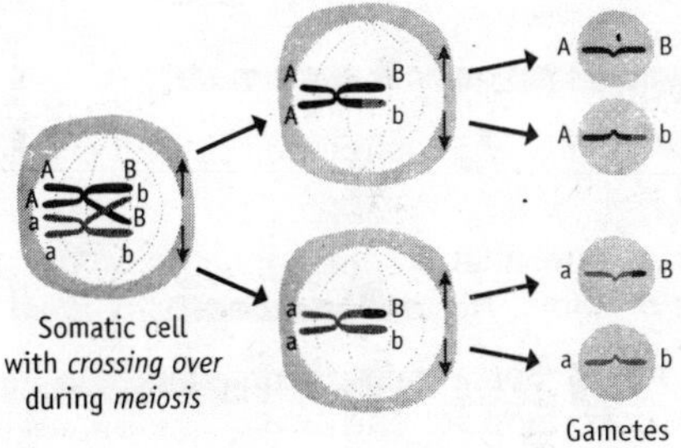

The frequency of recombinant offspring (ie. those formed from a gamete with *crossing over* (Ab or aB) is used in *chromosome mapping*.

mapping See *chromosome mapping*.

meiosis is division of *diploid* cells to produce *haploid* cells, usually ova (egg) and sperm. During *meiosis* the number of chromosomes is halved, so *meiosis* is referred to as reduction division. Stages occurring during meiosis are shown in the figure.

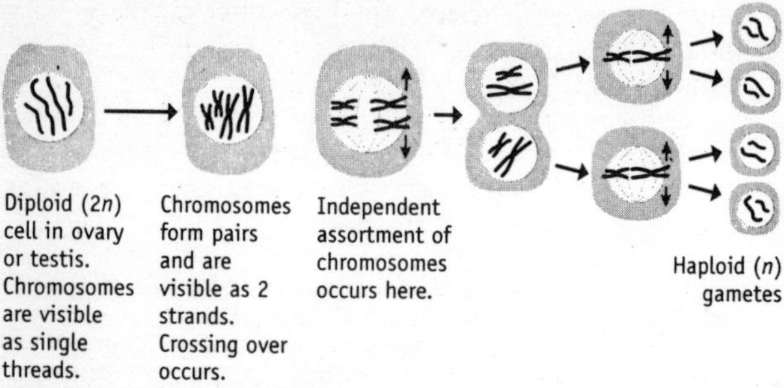

mitochondrion (plural, mitochondria) An *organelle* where respiration occurs. It supplies the cell with energy for chemical reactions.

mutagen A factor that produces mutations. See *Chapter 2, Blueprint of Life B, Heredity and DNA, mutation.*

multiple alleles Some traits are determined by more than two alleles. As there are only two chromosomes of each type in a cell, there will be only two alleles present at one time.

Examples of multiple allele inheritance are;

- A-B-O *blood groups in humans* are determined by 3 alleles A, B and O.
- Eye colour in the fruit fly, *Drosophila*. About 24 different alleles have been discovered. Normal red eye colour is dominant and masks pigments produced by any of the

other alleles. When two of the other alleles occur together, they produce an intermediate eye colour.

- Fur colour in rabbits is controlled by 4 alleles. Allele C produces a fully coloured coat, the allele c^h, when homozygous produces a Himalayan pattern; c^{ch}, when homozygous, produces a chinchilla coat; and c, when homozygous, produces an albino. These alleles may be arranged in order to show dominance: C, c^h, c^{ch}, c. C is dominant and c is recessive to other alleles; c^h and c^{ch} are incompletely dominant.

mutation See *Chapter 2, Blueprint of Life B, Heredity and DNA*. Chromosome mutation occurs when:

- a large piece of chromosome, or a block of genes, breaks off and is rearranged, so that the base sequence is altered. This is called a block mutation and includes inversion, translocation, deletion and duplication;
- an homologous pair of chromosomes does not separate during *meiosis* (ie. non-disjunction). The zygote formed in fertilisation will have an extra chromosome. The individual will have three of a particular chromosome, instead of the normal two. This condition is called *trisomy*. A person with Down syndrome has 3 copies of chromosome 21;
- an organism has three or more sets of chromosomes (ie. polyploidy). Usually organisms are *diploid* ($2n$) and have two sets (homologous pairs). An organism with three sets of chromosomes will be triploid ($3n$). This condition is rare in animals, but more common in plants. It occurs when all the chromosomes move to the same pole, during *meiosis*, to form a *diploid* gamete. If this gamete unites with a normal *haploid* gamete in fertilisation, then a triploid individual will result.

Gene mutation is a small change, ranging from change in a single base to a whole gene; these include:

- base substitution (point mutation), where a single base may be replaced by another, to alter that one codon (triplet of bases responsible for one amino acid);
- frameshift mutation occurs when a base is deleted or inserted. This displaces the bases along the rest of the chromosome and alters the whole series of codons (a codon is a set of 3 bases).

Mutations occurring in *somatic cells* cannot be passed on to the offspring (eg. cancer) and are called somatic mutations. Those appearing in gametes are known as germ line mutations. They can be inherited and provide a source of variation in the population. Variations are important for natural selection and evolution.

organelle A structure inside a cell (eg. *chloroplast, mitochondrion)*.

plasmid A small piece of circular DNA found in organisms such as bacteria and yeast. They can duplicate independently of the other *chromosomes* and can be transferred between bacteria. *Plasmids* are useful in *recombinant DNA* technology.

polygenic inheritance occurs when the development of a trait is controlled by a number of genes. These traits usually appear as continuous or gradual variation in the population. (eg. height, skin colour in humans and colour of kernels in wheat or corn, seed size in beans). For instance height in humans is controlled by several genes, each contributing with an additive effect. For simplicity, consider three genes A, B and C, each contributing 5 cm to height. The recessive genes aabbcc produce the minimum height (eg. 100 cm). Genotype Aabbcc will produce an individual 105 cm tall, while an AAbbcc will be 110 cm and AABbCc 120 cm.

polyploidy describes an organism which has three or more sets of chromosomes. See *mutation*.

protein synthesis Proteins are built in ribosomes based on information provided by DNA. See *Chapter 2, Blueprint of Life B, Heredity and DNA*.

recombinants are offspring which have characteristics as a result of *crossing over* in *meiosis*. See *linked genes*. The frequency of recombinants in breeding experiments is used for *chromosome mapping*.

recombinant DNA is DNA which has been broken and a new piece of DNA inserted. It is produced during *crossing over* in *meiosis*. It is also produced in the laboratory, where genes are inserted into the DNA using *recombinant DNA* technology (also known as gene splicing). This produces new characteristics in the host, or enables the host to produce new proteins. For instance, the gene which codes for insulin may be removed from a host and inserted into bacteria. The bacteria will be able to produce large quantities of insulin which can be used in medical treatment.

Procedure: Bacteria are broken and DNA including *plasmids* is extracted. The DNA is centrifuged to separate the *plasmids* from the main chromosomes. Purified *plasmids* are exposed to *restriction enzymes*, which cut the DNA circle at a specific point. This leaves 'sticky ends' made up of unpaired bases. The DNA to be inserted is also treated with the same *restriction enzymes*, so that it has 'sticky ends' with bases complementary to that of the *plasmid* DNA. This donor DNA is joined into the *plasmid* using ligases. The new DNA circle or *recombinant DNA* (*plasmid*), is added to a medium containing bacteria. The bacteria pick up these free *plasmids* and add them to their genetic material. The DNA replicates precisely and is passed on to daughter bacterial cells for many generations. This copying process is known as gene cloning. These bacteria are now capable of producing large quantities of the required chemical. See *Chapter 8, Biotechnology, transgenetic organism.*

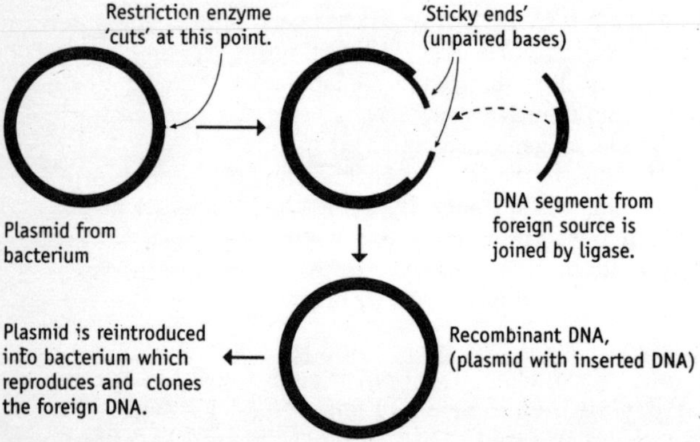

restriction enzymes These enzymes are capable of recognising a certain short length of DNA sequence and cutting at the point where it is found in the molecule (eg. the *restriction enzyme* called Sma I cuts CCGGG). *Restriction enzymes* are used to isolate, sequence and manipulate genes.

rhesus blood group See *blood groups in humans.*

RNA (ribonucleic acid) See *Chapter 2, Blueprint of Life B, Heredity and DNA*.

RNA polymerase is an enzyme which joins the RNA nucleotides in the order specified by the DNA during *transcription.*

selective breeding occurs when the breeder chooses the characteristics to be bred. Organisms with unwanted characteristics are discarded. In Australia, crops such as wheat have been bred to improve the quality of the grain and to increase its yield, as well as to produce plants which can withstand harsh environmental conditions and to resist disease. Selective breeding may change the genetic nature of species. See *Chapter 2, Blueprint of Life B, Heredity and DNA*.

somatic cell Any cell in the body except reproductive cells.

tissue culture See *Chapter 2, Blueprint of Life B, Heredity and DNA, cloning.*

translation of the genetic code occurs on the ribosomes. See *Chapter 2, Blueprint of Life B, Heredity and DNA, protein synthesis.*

transcription is the production of RNA from DNA. A single strand of DNA acts as a template for this synthesis. The RNA bases pair with their corresponding DNA bases, hence obtaining the genetic code needed for protein synthesis. See *Chapter 2, Blueprint of Life B, Heredity and DNA, protein synthesis.*

transposable DNA Segments of DNA can change their position within the chromosome or from one chromosome to another. This segment consists of one to several genes or control elements and is referred to as a transposable genetic element or transposon. The movement may involve complete excision from one site and insertion in another. Alternatively the segment may duplicate itself and leave a copy in the original site. These movements create new DNA sequences and may change *gene expression.*

trisomy See *mutation.*

whole animal cloning See *cloning.*

CHAPTER 7
The Human Story

absolute dating See *dating fossils.*

age of Earth See *geological time.*

***Australopithecus* (southern ape-man)** A genus of fossil *primates* with ape-like skulls and human-like jaws. Their *fossils* are dated at 2–4.5 million years and include *Australopithecus ramidus*, *A. afarensis*, *A. robustus*, *A. boisei*, (now known as *Paranthropus boisei*).

blood proteins See *haemoglobin.*

classification hierarchy (levels) Classification systems group all organisms into a number of kingdoms. Each kingdom is subdivided into phyla (singular, phylum), then classes, orders, families, genera (singular, genus) and species. The greatest number of organisms is found at the kingdom level. The most closely related organisms are found at the species level.

classification of humans

Classification level	Characteristics of this level
Kingdom - animal	Heterotrophic (no chloroplasts), no cell wall, mobile

Classification level		Characteristics of this level
Phylum	– chordate	Notochord; hollow, dorsal nerve cord
Class	– mammal	Hair, mammary glands, endothermic
Order	– primate	Opposable thumb, binocular vision, nails
Family	– hominidae	Forelimbs shorter than hindlimbs, upright stance, absence of tail, flat face, with nostrils close and pointed down.
Genus	– *Homo*	Nails flat, completely upright with bipedal gait, S-shaped spine, large brain
Species	– *Homo sapiens*	Very large cerebral cortex, ability to learn, speech.

clinal gradation is a gradual change of characteristics, reflecting a change in environmental conditions (eg. climate). For instance, people in hot climates are generally tall and thin, and the body shape can be seen to become gradually shorter and stockier as we move into cooler areas. It has occurred because of (i) overlapping geographic areas, (ii) immigration and invasion, (iii) improved transport and interaction, (iv) improved communication systems. See *polymorphism*.

contributions to the understanding of hominid evolution
An Australian anatomist Raymond Dart found a fossil in

1924 referred to as the 'missing link'. He found it at Taung in South Africa and called it *Australopithecus* ('southern ape-man'). It was later named *A. africanus* ('southern ape-man from Africa'). The two million year old fossil consisted of a skull and cast of the brain of a young chimp-like animal with human teeth. He hypothesised that its structure was intermediate between men and other living anthropoids.

Robert Broom, a Scottish palaeontologist (a scientist who studies fossils) joined Dart in his search for further information about human ancestry. They found adults, with human-like jaws and teeth. The vertebral columns and limbs suggested they were bipedal. In 1938 Broom found fossils which were similar to *A. africanus* but much stronger and more robust. These he called *A. robustus*.

Louis Leakey, his wife Mary and son Richard have made amazing and important discoveries including *A. boisei* (1959) and *H. habilis* (1964) in Africa. Maeve Leakey discovered *A. anamensis* (1995).

Jane Goodall is renowned for her work in the 1960s and 1970s with chimpanzees and their use of tools. This has provided an understanding of *primate* and *hominid* behaviour.

Don Johanson discovered *A. afarensis* ('Lucy') in 1974, the possible ancestor of other australopithecines and *Homo* species.

Philip Tobias, a colleague of Louis Leakey, was involved in the discovery of *Homo habilis ('handy man')* in 1964.

culture Human culture includes all aspects of human lifestyle such as behaviour, ideas, values, beliefs, traditions, social customs and work styles. Cultural development has meant a change in human relationship with the environment. Early humans began to control and modify the environment to help them survive. The diagram illustrates the sequence of the main events in cultural development.

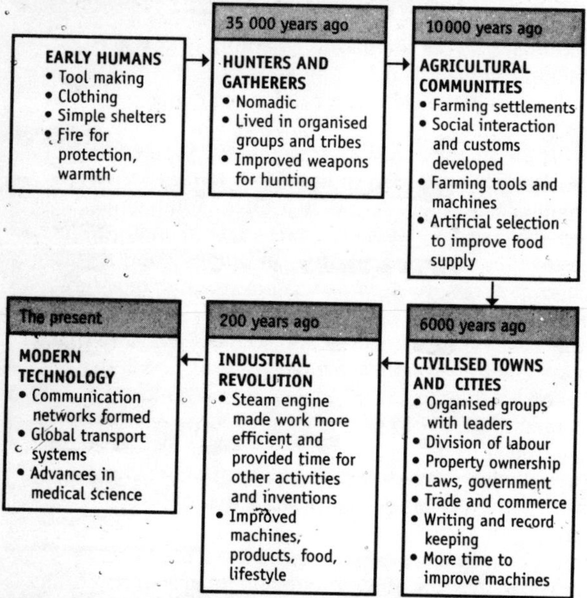

cultural development of humans and other primates

Comparison of *humans* with other *primates* shows an increased development in the use of tools, communications and social interactions.

- Tools and toolmaking have shown distinct change during the history of humans. Tools of early *primates* consisted of sticks and rocks. Early *humans* used chipping stones, hand-made tools shaped from wood, bone and ivory, and later, flint tools which had a hard sharp edge. They later developed metal tools and simple machines which improved their lifestyle and made them more efficient. This gave them time to design more complex machinery. Inventions led to the development of our modern day technology.

- Social interaction changed from the small tribal or 'family' groups of apes and early *humans* to large modern societies in cities. Group living increases survival: it provides protection from predators and increases the chances of reproduction. The hunter-gatherers needed to work in large, cooperative groups. Later, agricultural villages and stable settlements formed. Then towns and cities developed with complex activities, politics, laws and trading. Tasks were divided and individuals specialised in particular activities. This is called division of labour. It is an efficient social system as people can concentrate on learning and completing a few tasks well.
- Communication is needed in social systems and relationships (eg. hunters need to communicate to organise large hunts). In early *humans*, communication was by body language and speech, painting, symbols and later writing, which also provided a means of storing information. This eventually led to printing, so information could be spread and shared, and finally to today's televisions, phones, radios and computers. These have helped *humans* to take control of the surroundings.

dating fossils The age of *fossils* may be found by relative and absolute dating techniques.

- Relative dating techniques compare fossils with other known fossils or index fossils in the same layers (or strata) of rocks. This is known as stratigraphic correlation. (Strata = layers; correlation = comparing and matching.) Fossils in the same rocks must have been formed at the same time, so they are the same age. Fossils in lower layers of rocks are usually older than those nearer the surface. Rock layers in two cliff faces are compared in the figure.

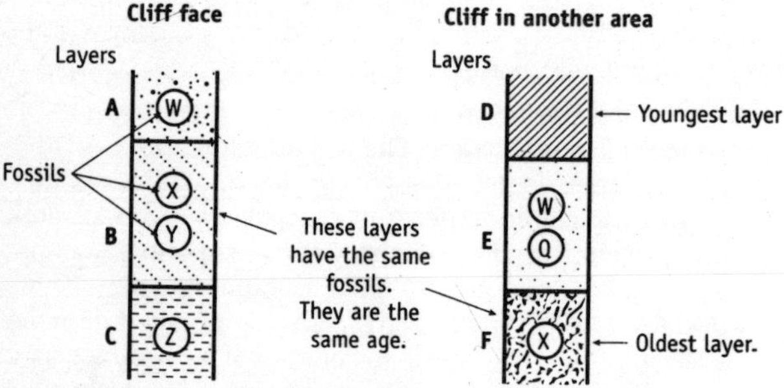

If rock layer B was formed 100 million years ago, then fossils X and Y must be 100 million years old. Fossil Z is below this and so must be older. Fossil W is in a younger layer of rock and so is a more recent fossil. In another area, Fossil Q is found in the same layer as W. W may be used to determine the age of Q.

- Absolute or radiometric dating is carried out using radioactive substances occurring naturally in organisms (eg. carbon-14), or rocks (uranium-238). These radioactive elements break down or decay at a known rate. For instance, uranium decays to form lead. By comparing the amount of uranium and lead in the rock, it is possible to work out the age of the rock. If there is only a little uranium left and a large accumulation of lead, the uranium has been decaying for a long time, so the rock must be very old. The half-life of uranium is 4.5 billion years. This means that in 4.5 billion years, 100 grams of uranium will have decayed so that only 50 g (half the original mass) remains.

determining relationships between primates may involve *karyotype* analysis, *DNA–DNA hybridisation,* comparison of *haemoglobins, DNA sequencing,* and *mitochondrial DNA* as molecular clocks.

diversity Humans show a large range of characteristics (*polymorphism*). Many of these characteristics overlap in different geographical areas and demonstrate *clinal gradation.* Different groups have been called subgroups or races. A race is a group of people living in the same geographic area and sharing a number of genetic characteristics not shared by other groups (eg. the epicanthic folds on the eyelids of Asian people). It is now difficult to support the concept of race because there has been considerable mixing of genes between the different gene pools since prehistoric times. Interbreeding causes mixing of genes in different populations. See origins of *Homo sapiens*.

DNA See *Chapter 2, Blueprint of Life B, Heredity and DNA*.

DNA–DNA hybridisation is used to determine relationships between *species*. DNA of closely related *species* will have a similar nucleotide base order. Single strands of DNA (polynucleotides) of closely related species will combine and bond readily to form hybrid DNA. *DNA hybridisation* involves splitting the DNA molecule lengthwise to expose the nucleotide bases. Segments of DNA from different species are added. If the base pairs match and bind readily and strongly, then the two organisms are close relatives. Heat is used to determine how strongly the bases are combined. *DNA–DNA hybridisation* has been used to find relationships between different *primates*.

DNA sequencing is the technique used to find the order of bases in the DNA molecule. Sequencing makes it possible to compare the DNA of different *species* and to determine how closely related two organisms are. Closely related individuals will have a very similar order of nucleotide bases. See *DNA–DNA hybridisation*.

evolutionary relationships Different types of evidence have been used to determine relationships between *primates* and how modern *humans* evolved. These include *fossils*, comparative anatomy and biochemical studies such as analysis of *blood proteins* and DNA. Many fossils of early humans (*Homo*) and ape-like hominids (*Australopithecus*) have been found, but it is difficult to determine which ones are related. The changes from one *species* to the next are not very smooth. New *species* seem to appear and disappear, and it is difficult to work out relationships.

Scientists have proposed family trees to show possible evolutionary pathways. The fossil evidence provides confusing information and is open to interpretation. There are many gaps in the *hominid* fossil record and new finds are still occurring. As new information is collected, scientists change their ideas. Louis Leakey and his son Richard Leakey put forward the following possible evolutionary pathways with fossil information which was available in the 1960s and 1970s.

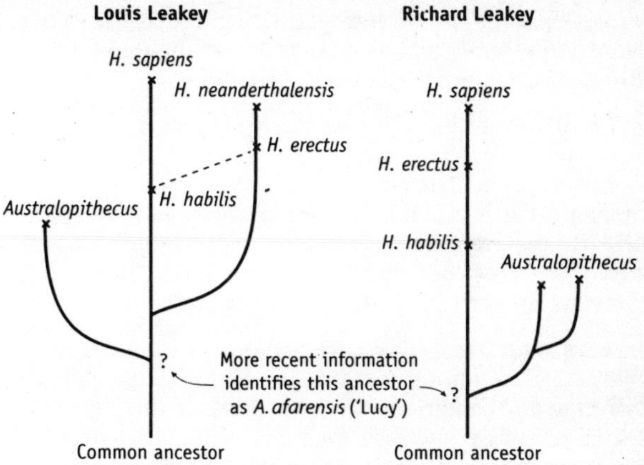

The following family tree shows possible relationships of *hominid* fossil species mentioned in the course.

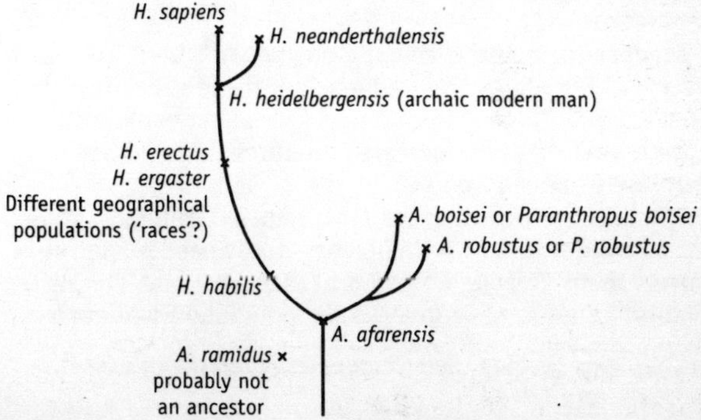

A. ramidus does not seem to fit into the tree; it has been discovered recently and its relationship to the other Australopithecines has not been determined.

fossils are the remains of past life. They may be preserved whole specimens, hard parts (such as bones), casts, moulds, imprints, burrows, petrified specimens or droppings. For fossils to form, organisms need to be quickly buried so that they are not eaten by scavengers and do not decay. They are generally formed under water. The sediments in which they are buried need to be undisturbed.

future trends in the evolution of humans In a natural situation, the organism that is best adapted to the environmental conditions survives. *Humans* can control their environment and hence *human* evolution.

With *genetic engineering* and information supplied by the *Human Genome Project*, *humans* are able to change their gene pool and direct human evolution. This technology and information enables humans to select characteristics for the population.

Modern medicine is keeping people with harmful genes alive and breeding. The frequency of these genes is increasing in the population and may affect evolution.

Increased mobility increases interbreeding and leads to a decrease in *polymorphism*.

Humans are polluting the environment. Pollutants may become the future selecting factor unless people control or correct them. People intolerant to them may die. People with tolerant genes may survive, so the population will evolve.

genetic engineering See *Chapter 2, Blueprint of Life B, Heredity and DNA*.

geological time By using *fossil* information, and dating the rocks surrounding them it is possible to form a history of life on Earth. Earth is estimated to be 4500 million years old and the age of the earliest traces of life has been estimated at 3500 million years. Geological time since life began has been divided into four eras, from the oldest, the Precambrian, through the Palaeozoic and the Mesozoic to the most recent, the Cainozoic. Eras are subdivided into periods, and periods into epochs.

haemoglobin is the protein in red blood cells, responsible for oxygen transport. Proteins are composed of long chains of amino acids, in specific numbers and order. Closely related species will have a very similar order of bases in the DNA. The base sequence determines the order of amino acids in proteins; hence closely related species will have a similar order of the amino acids in a specific protein (eg. haemoglobin). The amino acid sequence in haemoglobin has been successfully compared in different species and used to determine their relationships.

hominid A *primate* belonging to the family Hominidae. Hominids include *humans* (genus *Homo*) and *fossils* with some *human* characteristics (genus *Australopithecus*, *Paranthropus*). See *classification of humans*.

hominid fossils Information about *hominids*, mentioned in the course, from oldest to most recent, is given in the figures.

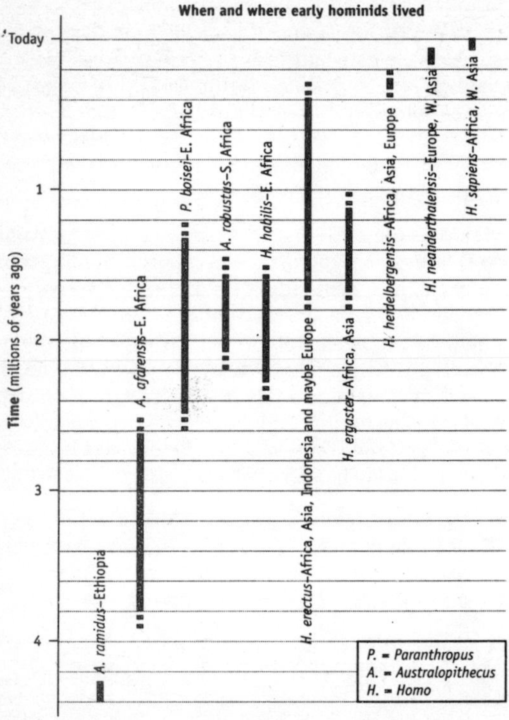
When and where early hominids lived
Today
1
2
3
4
Time (millions of years ago)
A. ramidus–Ethiopia
A. afarensis–E. Africa
P. boisei–E. Africa
A. robustus–S. Africa
H. habilis–E. Africa
H. erectus–Africa, Asia, Indonesia and maybe Europe
H. ergaster–Africa, Asia
H. heidelbergensis–Africa, Asia, Europe
H. neanderthalensis–Europe, W. Asia
H. sapiens–Africa, W. Asia
P. = Paranthropus
A. = Australopithecus
H. = Homo

*A. = *Australopithecus*	**P. = *Paranthropus*	***H. = *Homo*

Hominid	Age (approx. beginning of existence)	Structure	Height	Brain size	[illegible]
**A. ramidus*	4.5 million years	Only fragments found. Bipedal	——	——	——
A. afarensis	4 million years	Light build; 30–60 kg Ape-like face, human-like teeth, curved fingers and toes	100–150 cm	400–500 cm^3	Probably made and used tools
***P. boisei*	2.6 million years	Very heavy build 40–80 kg, long arms. Crest on skull	120–140 cm	410–530 cm^3	Vegetarian
P. robustus or A. robustus	2.2 million years	Heavy build 40–80 kg, long arms. Crest on skull	110–130 cm	530 cm^3	Vegetarian
****H. habilis*	2 million years	40 kg Small face with nose. Small teeth, eyebrow ridges, no chin	100 cm	500–650 cm^3	Stone tools, hunters, shelters
H. erectus	1.8 million years	Strong, robust. Thick skull, large eyebrow ridges, smaller teeth	130–170 cm	750–1250 cm^3	Hunter-gatherers, stone and bone tools, used fire. Lived in cooperative groups

continued

*A. = *Australopithecus* **P. = *Paranthropus* ***H. = *Homo*

Hominid	Age (approx. beginning of existence)	Structure	Height	Brain size	Inferred culture
H. ergaster	Similar to *H. erectus*. Believed to be a different geographical population				
H. heidelbergensis (archaic *H. sapiens*)	400 000 years	Robust and human-like. Flat face, definite nose	150 cm	1100–1400 cm^3	———
H. neanderthalensis	150 000 years	Robust, human-like. Reduced eyebrow ridges. Nose, some with chin. Teeth small	150–170 cm	1200–1750 cm^3	Simple shelters, clothes, necklaces, burial, tools, hunters
H. sapiens	80 000 years	Small or no eyebrow ridge. Chin developed. Upright forehead	160–185 cm	1200–1700 cm^3	Metal tools, agriculture, domestication of animals, villages

hominid fossils difficult to classify Many *hominid fossils* are difficult to classify, as classification is based on relationships and these are often unclear. Neanderthal Man lived at the same time as early *Homo sapiens* (modern *humans*) and was very similar in many ways. These people had an advanced lifestyle and body structure. They were adapted to cold climates and their build suggests that they were extremely hard-workers. They used carefully crafted tools, had a high degree of social interaction and performed burial ceremonies. They were originally classified as a subspecies of *H. sapiens* and were classified as *Homo sapiens* *neanderthalensis*. DNA analysis of Neanderthal remains indicates that they are not ancestors of *H. sapiens*.

Homo is a genus of *primates* with *human* characteristics. See *classification of humans*. It includes *Homo sapiens* (modern *humans*), *H. neanderthalensis*, *H. heidelbergensis*, *H. erectus*, *H. ergaster*, *H. habilis*.

Human Genome Project See *Chapter 6, Option, Genetics: The Code Broken?* The sequence of the nucleotides in human DNA has been described, thus forming the basis to link the approximately 30 000 human genes with places on the chromosomes. This technology would allow genetic screening. Then undesirable foetuses could be aborted, and insurance companies and work places might refuse people of certain make-up.

human populations Modern technology has made life safer and easier so that more people survive and reproduce. There are better treatments for disease and improved health programs. Agricultural research and *genetic engineering* have improved stock, crops and food supplies. As a result the population has increased dramatically, causing problems with food shortage, pollution, poverty, housing and stress.

humans Members of the genus *Homo*. They are mammals in the Order Primates. They belong to the Family Hominidae and are separated from other *primates* (such as the apes and monkeys) because of distinguishing features such as upright stance, and large brain. *Humans* are the most highly developed *primates*. They have an extended period of the juvenile stage (about 15 years) during which parents care for them. Social groups are much larger and have a greater degree of specialisation in tasks. Humans have developed much more complicated tools and technology and are able to use them. Communication systems are more complex and cover larger distances, conveying more complex information. See *classification of humans*.

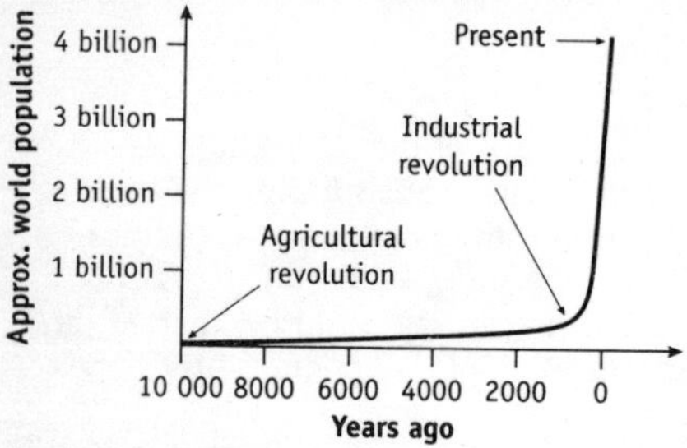

This population explosion has increased poverty, famine, disease, and pollution, and is exhausting food, clothing, and housing.

interpreting the fossil record It is often difficult to interpret data about the past from *fossils* alone because (1) There are gaps in the record. Often conditions are not suitable for the formation of *fossils*. Once formed they may have been disturbed and destroyed by earth movements and volcanic activity, or they remain undiscovered. (2) The accuracy of *fossil dating* may vary depending on the technology used. The half-life of uranium is very long and does not allow a very accurate estimate. Carbon-14 on the other hand is accurate but can be used for dating tissues of organisms only up to 50 000 years old. Older *fossils* need to be dated from the surrounding rocks. (3) Information obtained from *fossils* is open to interpretation. The structure and lifestyle of an ancient animal may be determined from a few *fossil* remains. This involves interpretation using comparisons with present-day organisms.

karyotype The complete set of chromosomes in a cell. It is prepared from white blood cells in the metaphase stage of mitosis and provides the number and appearance (shape, size and banding). It is shown by a photograph or diagram which has the chromosome pairs lined up in order of size. Two organisms in the same species have the same karyotype, but the chromosome number may vary considerably between closely related species.

molecular clock See *mitochondrial DNA*.

mitochondrial DNA Most DNA is found in the nucleus. Mitochondria have their own DNA and genes. It is almost always circular and is attached to the inner membrane of the organelle. Replication of this DNA is independent of DNA in the nucleus and it is inherited only from the mother, making it easier to trace evolutionary pathways. The DNA in mitochondria mutates at a known rate, so these mutations can be used as *molecular clocks*. They make it possible to compare species and to see how long ago organisms had a common ancestor. The more mutations present, the more time has passed since their common ancestor existed and the more distantly related they are.

Multiregional model One hypothesis of how human races originated. It is based on *fossils* and comparison of anatomy. The model proposes that 1 million years ago, *Homo erectus* populations in Africa moved into Asia and Europe. Once they had spread, they evolved gradually in many different regions throughout the world to form the different types of *H. sapiens*. This suggests that *H. sapiens* originated in many different places or regions. The different characteristics which had evolved in *H. erectus* in different regions persisted through to modern *humans*. This is known as *regional continuity*. Compare with *Out of Africa model*.

origins of *Homo sapiens* It is believed that human ancestors originated in south-east Africa and because of their nomadic lifestyle spread out through Europe and Asia. Groups became isolated geographically and lived in different environmental conditions. As a result they evolved independently. Because of natural selection, each population developed characteristics suitable for its particular environment and lifestyle. See *Blueprint of Life, A Evolution, natural selection*.

Two different ideas have been put forward to explain where *H. sapiens* originated. The *Out of Africa model* and the *Multiregional model* (regional continuity).

Out of Africa model This suggests that *Homo sapiens* evolved 200 000 years ago in Africa and then, once evolved, spread out through Asia and Europe, replacing archaic populations. This means that the origin of *H. sapiens* can be traced back to one location. *H. sapiens* was better adapted to the environment, eventually replacing archaic populations of early *Homo*. Studies using *mitochondrial DNA* support this hypothesis. DNA in Africans shows more mutation than elsewhere. This suggests that *H. sapiens* has been in Africa longer than elsewhere. Compare with *Multiregional model*.

polymorphism (poly = many; morphism = forms). *Homo sapiens* exists as different groups with distinctly different characteristics. *Humans* are said to show *polymorphism* (eg. different skin pigmentation, or stocky or slim build). Pigment, called melanin, is produced in the outer layers of the skin. It shields and protects the lower tissues from damage by ultraviolet sunlight. People near the equator have this dark protective skin. Pale skin is an advantage to people living in overcast places. It allows them to collect sufficient sunlight to produce vitamin D which is needed for the growth of healthy bones. Stocky build is commonly found in people in cooler climates. It provides a small surface area to volume ratio so that they do not radiate and lose too much heat. Tall, slim people have a large surface area to volume ratio. This enables them to radiate excess heat and keep cool in warmer climates.

Primates An order of mammals that includes the prosimians, monkeys, apes and *humans*. These organisms share a number of characteristics: opposable thumb and toe for grasping; nails; pads on fingertips; flexible wrists and shoulders; large forebrain with the area for smell reduced and the area for vision enhanced; snout reduced; stereoscopic and colour vision; social groups; long period of gestation (foetal development); single births, prolonged childhood and parental care. *Primate* groups and characteristics are shown in the figure (on page 140).

• The characteristics of *primates* vary considerably, depending on their lifestyle. For instance, New World monkeys (eg. the spider monkeys) live in trees. They have a prehensile (or grasping) tail and long fingers to hold on to branches. Old World monkeys (eg. baboons) do not have a prehensile tail; they spend their time on the ground, foraging for food. Other tree-dwelling *primates* have an opposable toe to grasp branches. *Humans* need a big toe to help support an upright stance.

Two *primates*, ape and human, are compared in the figure (on page 141).

Primates

- **Prosimians**
  - In Madagascar
  - Opposable big toe, small pointed snout, eyes forward, binocular vision
  - Tree dwellers
  - eg. lemur, tarsier
- **Anthropoids** (monkeys, apes, humans)
  - **Hominoids** (humans and apes)
    - **Lesser apes**
      - In Asia
      - Long arms, broad-chested, slender build
      - Can stand and walk upright, tree gymnasts
      - eg. gibbon, siamangs
    - **Greater apes**
      - In Africa and Asia
      - Large body, no tail, knuckle walkers
      - Use tools, advanced social groups
      - Ground dwellers, sleep in trees
      - eg. orangutan, chimpanzee, gorilla
    - **Hominids**
      - ***Australopithecus***
        - In Africa
        - Ape-like skulls, human-like limbs, generally bipedal
        - Ground dwellers
        - eg. *A. afarensis* ('Lucy')
      - ***Homo***
        - Africa, Asia, Europe and now world wide
        - Flat face, reduced brow ridges, chin, bipedal
        - Ground dwellers
        - eg. *H. neanderthalensis*
  - **Monkeys**
    - **New World monkeys**
      - In South America
      - Prehensile tail, wide nostrils
      - Tree dwellers
      - eg. howler and spider monkeys
    - **Old World monkeys**
      - In Africa and Asia
      - Tail not prehensile, nostrils close together and open downwards, callosites (pads to sit on) present
      - Ground dwellers
      - eg. baboon, macaque

Comparison of Ape and Human

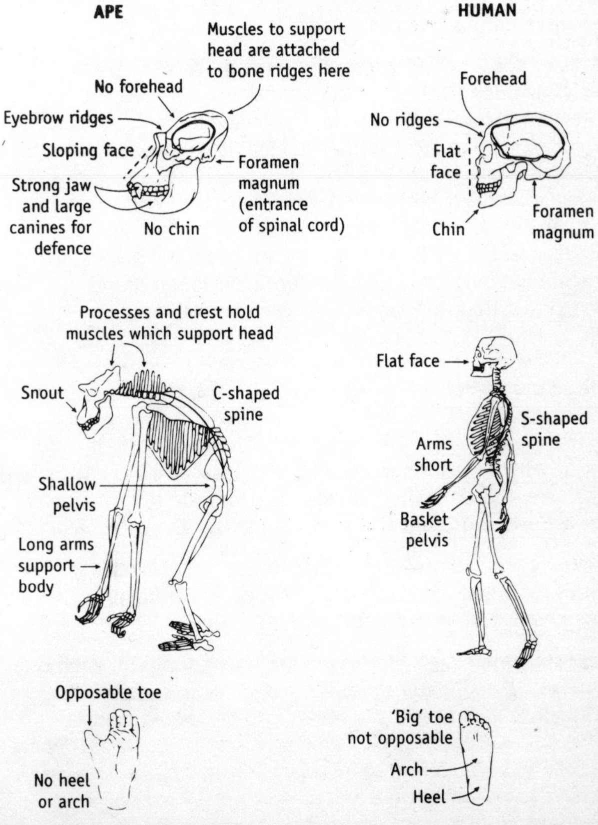

regional continuity See *Multiregional model.*

relative dating See *dating fossils.*

role of two hominid species in tracing evolutionary relationships *Australopithecus afarensis*, also called Lucy, was the oldest Australopithecine fossil found at the time of its discovery in 1974, in East Africa. It was estimated to have lived 2.9 to 3.9 million years ago. There was also a spectacular find of 13 similar individuals in one site. *A. afarensis* has a light build, with long arms and curved fingers and ape-like face and head. Teeth and jaws tend to be human-like. Donald Johanson, who found them, suggested that they are the ancestors of other later Australopithecines and the *Homo* species. *Homo heidelbergensis* is also known as Archaic *H. sapiens* and may be as old as 800 000 years. Many examples were found in North Spain, Africa and Asia. They show a mixture of ancient and modern features, with changes in the lower skull which may be associated with the voice box. Structural features and their time of existence indicate that they may be ancestors of both *H. neanderthalensis* and *H. sapiens*.

species Two organisms belong to the same species if they can interbreed naturally and produce fertile offspring, or if they have a common gene pool.

stereoscopic vision Both eyes are facing forward, each one producing a silightly different image of the same object. Therefore distance of the object can be judged (three-dimensional vision). This type of vision is important for tree dwellers, hunters and manipulators with fingers. Other animals (eg. rabbit) have their eyes on the side of their head, providing a very large field of vision for the early detection of predators.

Chapter 8

Biochemistry

ADP (adenosine diphosphate) See *coenzymes* and *ATP*.

action spectrum The wavelengths of *light* (colours) in which *photosynthesis* occurs. See *absorption spectrum* and *light*.

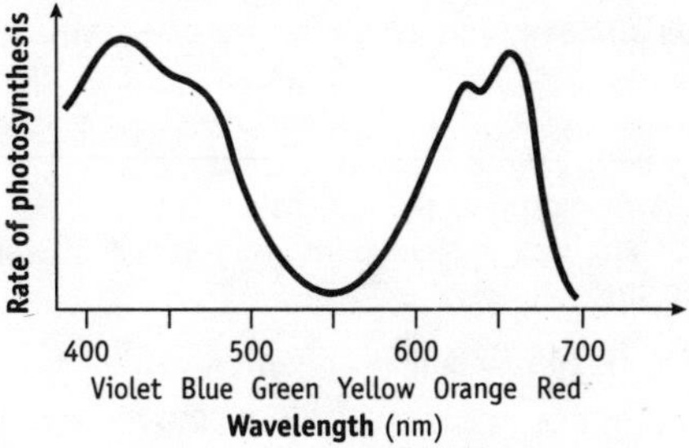

absorption spectrum. Light-sensitive pigments can absorb particular wavelengths (colours) of *light*. The absorption spectrum in the diagram on page 144 indicates the wavelengths of light absorbed by *chlorophyll*. The *absorption spectrum* of *chlorophyll* is slightly different from the *action spectrum* of *photosynthesis*. This suggests that other pigments are also involved in *photosynthesis*. The orange and yellow carotenoids absorb other wavelengths and pass the energy onto *chlorophyll* for use in *photosynthesis*.

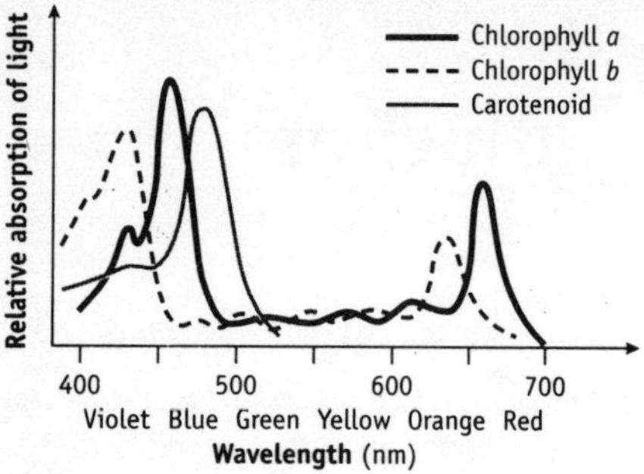

anoxygenic photosynthesisers *Photosynthesis* in some bacteria is different from that in green plants. *Chlorophyll a* is missing and *photosystem II* is lacking. As a result oxygen is not liberated. This is known as *anoxygenic photosynthesis*. Some of these organisms use sulfur compounds such as hydrogen sulfide instead of water; they produce sulfur instead of oxygen.

carbon dioxide + hydrogen sulfide
→ glucose + water + sulfur

$$CO_2 + 2H_2S \rightarrow (CH_2O) + H_2O + 2S$$

Other bacteria use hydrogen gas and produce water instead of oxygen.

ATP (adenosine triphosphate) is a molecule composed of adenine attached to a ribose sugar and three phosphate groups, bonded in sequence (AP ~ P ~ P). The phosphate groups are linked by high energy phosphodiester bonds.

Energy is released when the third phosphate group is separated from the molecule. This is used by the chemical reactions of the cells in all living things. When the phosphate bond is broken to release energy, *ADP* (adenosine diphosphate) is formed. (ATP $\rightarrow$ ADP + P + energy). *ADP* may be converted to *ATP* if it is supplied with phosphate groups and energy. This process is called *phosphorylation*. The energy for this reaction comes from respiration. See *coenzymes* and *photophosphorylation*.

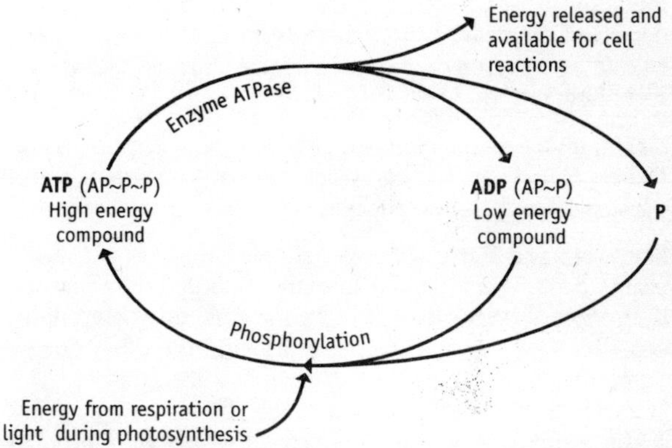

autotrophs are organisms that can synthesise their own food (organic compounds, rich in energy) from raw materials (inorganic compounds). The organic compounds formed may then be used to manufacture substances needed for body tissues. For instance, sugars formed in *photosynthesis* may be used to make amino acids and lipids. There are two main types of autotrophs: (1) photosynthetic autotrophs — those that obtain energy from sunlight to produce food (ie. organic material for growth and metabolism). Green plants and some bacteria are photosynthetic autotrophs; (2) chemosynthetic autotrophs — those that make food by using energy obtained from chemical reactions, instead of sunlight. Certain bacteria convert ammonia to nitrites. Some convert nitrites to nitrates, while others convert sulfides to sulfates, or methane to methanol. They use the energy obtained during these conversions to synthesise food needed for growth and metabolism. For instance, bacteria living in rift valleys in the depths of the ocean where there is no light use hydrogen sulfide as a source of energy to convert carbon dioxide to carbohydrates.

biochemistry is the study of chemical reactions in living things. It includes the chemical reactions occurring during *photosynthesis* and respiration.

Blackman and Mathgal (1895) showed that gas exchange in plants occurs through the stomates. In 1905 they reasoned that *photosynthesis* occurs in two stages; one being light sensitive (*light dependent reaction*), and the other not involving light, but limited by temperature. It was postulated that carbon dioxide could be incorporated into plant tissue without light but factors which were produced in the light-sensitive stage were required.

Experimentation shows that increasing the light also increases the rate of *photosynthesis* until a particular light intensity. Then a further increase in light has no effect on the photosynthesis rate. Because *photosynthesis* involves many enzymes, temperature will also affect the rate at which it occurs.

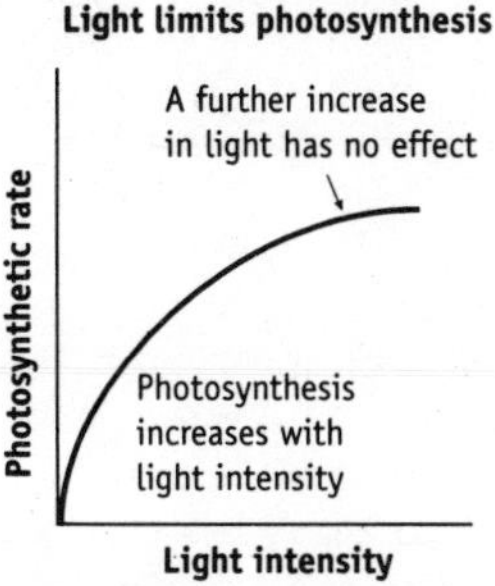

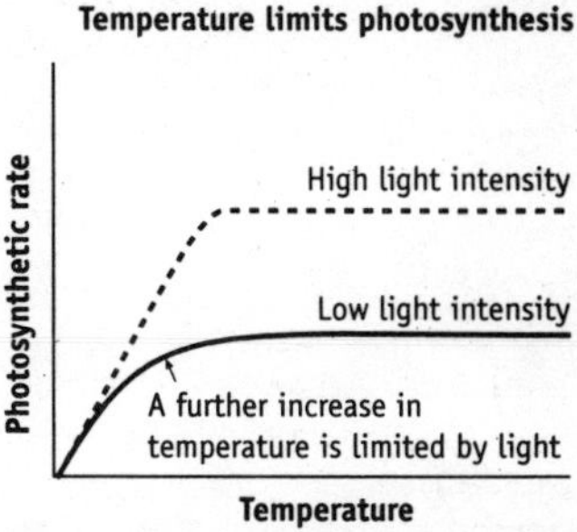

Calvin, Melvin (1946) outlined the pathway of the *light independent reaction* in *photosynthesis*. He used the carbon *isotope*, C-14, to label the carbon dioxide supplied to algae. The photosynthetic reaction was stopped at numerous points and intermediate products separated by *chromatography.* Calvin used X-ray techniques to identify and determine the order of the intermediate products in the chemical reactions. Calvin won the Nobel Prize in 1961 for this work. See *Calvin cycle.*

C-14 (carbon 14) See *Ruben and Kamen* and *Calvin, Melvin.*

Calvin cycle (also known as the *light independent reaction,* carbon fixation and dark reaction). The second stage of *photosynthesis* in which carbon dioxide (a low-energy compound) is converted to glucose (a high energy compound). This part of *photosynthesis* does not need *light.* It occurs in the stroma of the *chloroplast*. The series of complex steps involved was determined by *Calvin.* Carbon dioxide combines with an acceptor molecule, a 5-carbon sugar called ribulose biphosphate. Phosphoglycerate (PGA), 3-carbon sugar, is formed. PGA is phosphorylated by ATP and reduced by NADPH, both from the *light dependent reaction*, to form glyceraldehyde phosphate (PGAL). Most of the PGAL is used to form more of the original acceptor molecule, ribulose biphosphate. The rest of the PGAL is used to form glucose and then other carbohydrates.

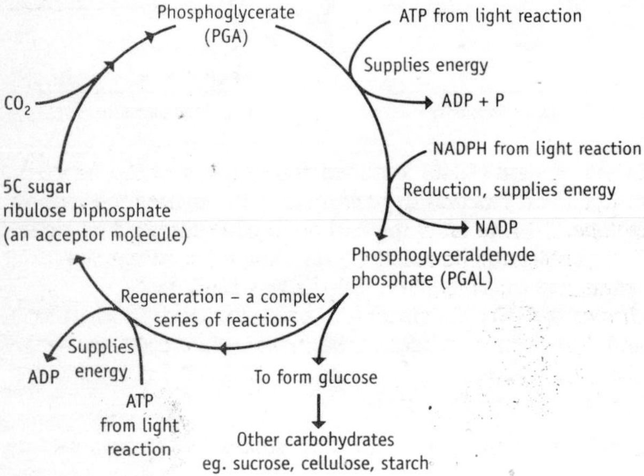

centrifugation See *homogenisation and centrifugation*.

chloroplasts are *organelles* found in the cytoplasm of cells of green plants. They are the sites of *photosynthesis*. Generally each 'green' cell contains between 20 and 100 *chloroplasts*, although some algae may have only one. Inside the *chloroplasts* are membranous, hollow discs called *thylakoids* which form stacks known as *grana*. The green pigment *chlorophyll* is found on the surfaces of the *thylakoids*. The grana are connected to each other by lamellae. The grana are surrounded by a granular matrix (or fluid) called stroma. The stroma contains DNA, ribosomes, lipid droplets and starch granules. Chloroplasts are seen as spherical bodies under the light microscope. A transmission electron microscope is needed to see the internal structures. Generally, *chloroplast* size in higher plants is about 5 microns (5×10^{-3} mm, 5 μm).

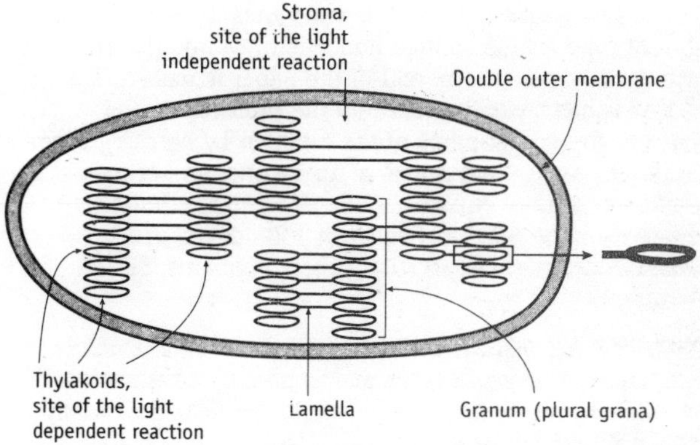

chlorophyll is a group of light-sensitive pigments found in *chloroplasts* and giving plants their green colour. It is generally composed of *chlorophyll a* and *chlorophyll b*. Together with other pigments, the carotenoids, it is responsible for the absorption of the light energy required for *photosynthesis*. *Chlorophyll* is found in the membranes of the *thylakoids*. The pigments are dissolved in the lipid layer of the membrane and are in close contact with membrane proteins, forming a lipo-protein complex.

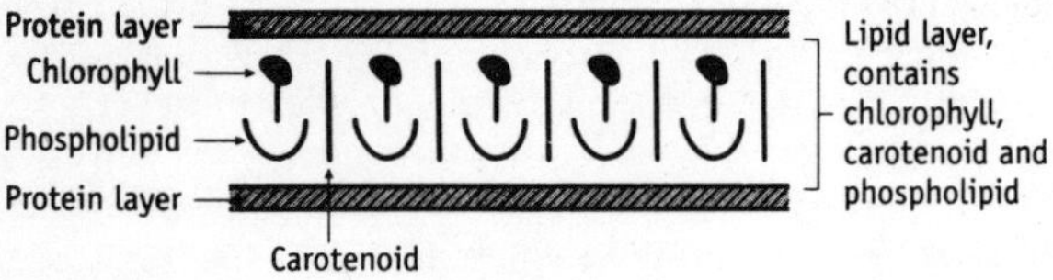

chromatography is used to separate the components of a mixture and analyse them. The substance to be analysed (eg. leaf pigment) is spotted and dried towards the end of a piece of filter paper. The end of the paper is placed in a suitable solvent which moves up the filter paper and separates the components of the pigment by carrying them at different rates. They travel at different rates because some are absorbed more strongly by the filter paper, inhibiting their movement. Mikhail Tswett in 1906 developed chromatography for separation of leaf pigments. See *chlorophyll.*

coenzymes are organic molecules required for enzymatic reactions such as *photosynthesis*. In *photosynthesis*, NADP and ADP are important *coenzymes*. In the *light dependent reaction* NADP (nicotinamide dinucleotide phosphate) accepts electrons (accompanied by protons) from the *electron transport chain* to form NADPH (reduced NADP). In the light reaction, energy released from the *electron transport chain* is used to convert ADP (adenine diphosphate) plus inorganic phosphate to high-energy *ATP*. (adenine triphosphate). The energy absorbed from the sun is stored as chemical energy in NADPH and *ATP*. Both substances drive the light independent phase, where carbon dioxide reacts to form sugar.

de Saussure, Nicolas Theodore (1804) concluded that water is necessary for *photosynthesis*. He weighed an enclosed plant and its surrounding air before and after *photosynthesis*. The increase in weight of the plant was greater than the gas used. He concluded that the rest of the plant's weight came from water. He indicated the interdependence of oxygen formation and carbon dioxide uptake and also showed that they both require light. He made the first quantitative measurements of *photosynthesis*.

electron transport chain A complex series of reactions occurring in the *light dependent reaction* in *photosynthesis*. When the *chlorophyll* molecule is activated by light, it passes high-energy electrons along a chain to acceptor molecules. Energy is released along the chain. See *photophosphorylation*.

Emerson and Arnold; Gaffron and Wahl (1930s) The experimental research of Emerson and Arnold and the interpretation of this research by Gaffron and Wahl led to the concept of the *photosynthetic unit*. Algae were exposed to microsecond flashes of light and the oxygen produced was measured. They found that one molecule of oxygen is produced by about 2500 *chlorophyll* molecules. It was hypothesised that a *photosynthetic unit* consists of *chlorophyll* and photoenzyme molecules and that light energy is transferred to reaction centres where it is involved in chemical reactions.

Engelmann, Thomas (1882) used ingenious experiments to determine the wavelengths of coloured *light* which were most effective in *photosynthesis.* With the help of Carl Zeiss, an optical instrument-maker, he projected the *spectrum* of visible light onto a thread of spirogyra (a microscopic, filamentous alga). He added bacteria, which migrate towards oxygen, ie. they migrate to areas where photosynthesis occurs. Bacteria moved to and concentrated in the red and blue lights, indicating sites of *photosynthesis.*

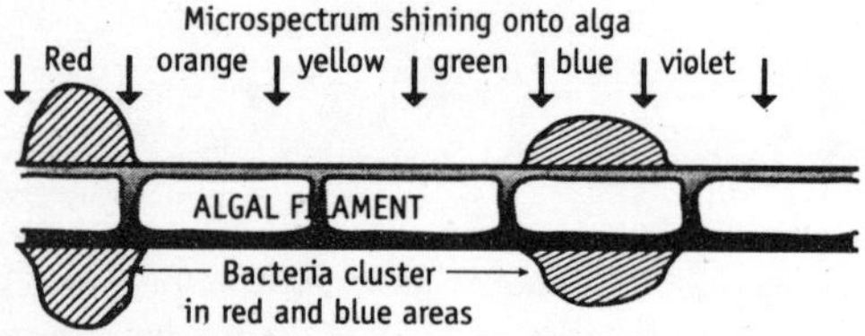

Engelmann's work led to the description of the *action spectrum.*

glyceraldehyde phosphate See *Calvin cycle.*

greenhouse effect. Carbon dioxide increases in the atmosphere as a result of pollution and the continued burning of fossil fuels. The accumulated carbon dioxide absorbs heat, reducing the amount that would normally be radiated. As a result a greenhouse effect occurs, increasing the temperature on the earth's surface. Plants use carbon dioxide in *photosynthesis* and may be used to control this greenhouse effect.

Hales, Stephen (1727) worked with gases and speculated that plants use part of the air for their nutrition and to form matter.

half-life See *isotope.*

homogenisation and centrifugation Homogenisation is the process used to break up cells so that their contents may be isolated and studied. Cells are carefully ground in a dilute buffer sugar solution. Many of the organelles, eg. *chloroplasts*, remain intact and can then be separated from the rest of the cell contents by placing the ground material in a centrifuge spinning at a high speed. To collect *chloroplasts*, the solution is centrifuged at a particular speed so that heavy particles such as starch grains, nuclei and pieces of cell wall settle to the bottom of the centrifuge tube. The liquid containing the *chloroplasts* and other light components is decanted and centrifuged again at a higher speed, so that *chloroplasts* settle to the bottom and other light particles remain in suspension and can be removed.

Hill and Scarisbruck (1937) worked with isolated *chloroplasts*. Experiments showed that *chloroplasts*, in the absence of carbon dioxide, produce oxygen. This indicated that the oxygen was liberated from water. The quantity of oxygen produced was consistent with the amount of water added. This research was confirmed by the work of *Ruben and Kamen* using *radioisotopes.*

history of photosynthesis Processes involved in plant growth were unknown until the 17th and 18th centuries. During this time investigations by *van Helmont, Hales, Priestly, Ingen-Housz, Senebier* and *de Saussure* and *Mayer* established the basics of *photosynthesis.* Their research, combined, showed that water, carbon dioxide and light energy produce oxygen and organic matter.

Ingen-Housz, Jan (1779) showed the importance of light for *photosynthesis*. He demonstrated that the green parts of plants could 'restore bad air' (ie. release oxygen in photosynthesis) only if the sun was shining. This was also related to the clearness of the day and exposure to the sun. He suggested that, in *photosynthesis*, light splits carbon dioxide to release oxygen. The remaining carbon is used to make plant matter. This is now known to be incorrect; the oxygen is produced by water.

$$CO_2 + H_2\underline{O} \rightarrow \underline{O}_2 + (CH_2O) + H_2O$$

isotopes Atoms of the same element existing in different forms containing different numbers of neutrons and consequently having a different mass (eg. oxygen has 8 protons and 8 neutrons and is called O-16. O-18 has 2 extra neutrons and is radioactive). Isotopes of some elements are unstable and emit radiation as they decay to a more stable form. Isotopes are used to label chemicals so that they may be traced through biochemical pathways or through the body. They can be identified and distinguished from 'normal' atoms by weight-sensitive techniques such as mass spectromatry and centrifugation. Also, the radiation emitted can be tracked; the radioactive substance can be detected using X-ray film. Radioactive carbon, phosphorus, hydrogen and oxygen have been used to trace pathways in *photosynthesis*. For instance, carbon dioxide containing an isotope of carbon (C-14) can be detected in intermediate compounds by stopping photosynthesis at different time intervals.

Isotopes are also used to measure time and reaction rate. This involves the *half-life* which is the time it takes for half the atoms in the sample of radioactive material to decay. *Radioisotopes* have different half-lives (eg. the half-life of potassium 40 is 1.3×10^9 years while that of phosphorus 32 is 14 days). Isotopes used as timers in biochemical pathways need to have a short half-life so that research may be completed in a reasonable time. *Radioisotopes* used as tracers in living tissue need a short half-life so that the destructive radioactive substance is removed from the body quickly. See *Ruben and Kamen* and *Calvin*.

Kamen See *Ruben and Kamen*.

light See *Chapter 4, Option — Communication, light* and *electromagnetic radiation*.

light dependent reaction The first stage of *photosynthesis*, involving a complex series of chemical reactions. During this stage, *chlorophyll* 'traps' light energy and converts it to a stored energy supply in the form of *ATP* and NADPH. Both *ATP* and NADPH supply energy for the *light independent reaction* (*Calvin cycle*) in which carbon dioxide is converted to carbohydrates. There are two pathways, known as *photosystems I and II*, involved in the light reaction. Each has its own reaction centre (P680 and P700), pigment system and *electron transport chain*.

- *Photosystem I*. Light (wavelength 703 nm) striking *chlorophyll* 'energises' electrons which are collected by reaction centre P700. These high energy electrons are passed along an *electron transport chain* to *NADP* to form NADPH. Some of the energy liberated in the electron chain is used in the formation of *ATP*.
- *Photosystem II*. Light (wavelength 682 nm) 'energises' *chlorophyll* electrons. Some of these high energy electrons are passed along an electron chain to *Photosystem I*, while others stay in *Photosystem II*, where energy released along the electron chain is used to synthesise ATP. Water is split to form oxygen and to release more electrons, which replace those that have moved along the chain.

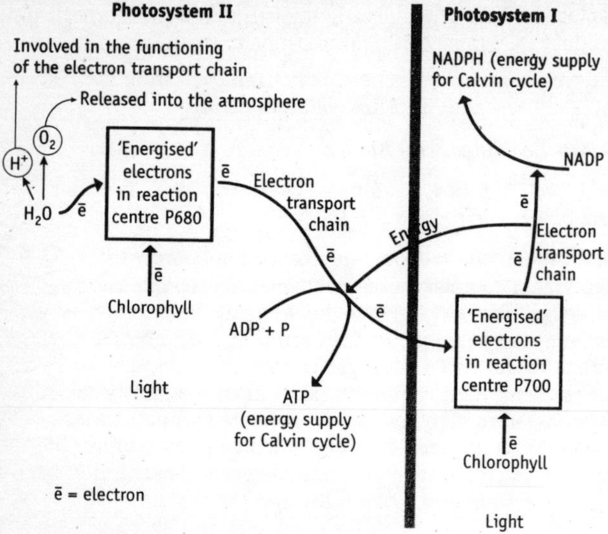

light independent reaction See *Calvin cycle.*

limiting factors in photosynthesis See *Blackman and Mathgal.*

Mayer See *von Mayer.*

NADP See *coenzymes.*

phosphoglycerate See *Calvin cycle.*

phosphorylation A phosphate group is added to a compound. See *ATP.*

photophosphorylation uses light energy in *photosynthesis* to produce *ATP* from ADP and phosphate. In the mid-20th century, Daniel Arnon and his colleagues demonstrated *photophosphorylation*; they isolated and illuminated *chloroplasts*, supplied with ADP and phosphate. The chloroplasts produced *ATP* and oxygen. *ATP* synthesis involves an electron transfer reaction occurring across membranes. The membrane makes possible an electrochemical gradient using the hydrogen ions (H^+)released from the water in *photosystem II*. In *photosynthesis*, when the *chlorophyll* molecule is activated by light, it donates high-energy electrons to acceptor molecules along a chain (called an *electron transport chain*). The chain reactions occur in the *thylakoid* membranes in the *chloroplast* and are believed to pass back and forth across the membranes. As the electrons move along the chain, some energy is released and is used to synthesise *ATP* from ADP and P. See *ATP* and *light dependent reaction*.

photosynthesis is a complex chemical reaction occurring in *chloroplasts* in plants. All living things depend on this process, as it uses the sun's energy to convert carbon dioxide and water into glucose and oxygen, used by organisms.

The overall reaction is:

$$6CO_2 + 12H_2O \xrightarrow[\text{chlorophyll}]{\text{Light and}} C_6H_{12}O_6 + 6O_2 + 6H_2O$$

Photosynthesis occurs in two stages, the *light dependent reaction* and the *light independent reaction* known as the *Calvin cycle*.

Study of *photosynthesis* is important because:

- it produces food so it can be used to increase crop yields. Possibly people will be able to artificially duplicate *photosynthesis* to increase food production;
- it may be used as a means of trapping solar energy which can then be converted to other forms of energy. This will decrease the use of non-renewable resources;
- it produces raw materials useful to humans (eg. timber, cork, rubber, food, oils, cotton);
- it uses carbon dioxide which may otherwise add to the *greenhouse effect*;
- it produces oxygen needed by organisms for respiration.

photosynthetic unit In *chloroplasts*, the *chlorophyll* and accessory pigments are organised into functional groups called *photosynthetic units*. Each unit comprises about 300 pigment molecules, including *chlorophyll a* and *b* and carotenoid. The pigment molecules act as antennae, responsive to light. One pigment molecule in the unit, a specialised form of *chlorophyll a*, acts as a reaction centre. There are two types of reaction centres, designated P680 and P700. They absorb light of different wavelengths. See *light dependent reaction.*

photosystems I and II See *light dependent reaction.*

pigments See *chlorophyll.*

Priestly, Joseph (1772) showed that plants could 'restore' air 'injured' by a burning candle (ie. plants produce oxygen and absorb carbon dioxide, while a candle produces carbon dioxide and absorbs oxygen). He showed that animals died when placed under a bell jar, but survived when a plant was placed under the jar as well. It is now known that this is because the plant produces oxygen that the animal can respire; the plant also removes excess carbon dioxide. Priestly discovered /produced oxygen when he heated mercury oxide.

radioisotope See *isotopes.*

reaction centre See *photosynthetic unit.*

Ruben and Kamen (1941) confirmed *van Niel's* proposal, and experiments of *Hill and Scarisbruck* that the **oxygen** released in *photosynthesis* comes from water rather than carbon dioxide as previously believed. Ruben and Kamen used water which had been labelled with a heavy *isotope* of oxygen, O-18, to trace the pathway of water in *photosynthesis* in algae. The carbon dioxide supplied had the common isotope of oxygen, O-16. They found that all the oxygen evolved was O-18 and hence came from the water.

In about 1940 Ruben and Kamen discovered radioactive carbon.(C-14) and recognised it as a useful tool for further research on *photosynthesis*. They demonstrated that plants exposed to carbon dioxide containing C-14 produced compounds containing this C-14.

Sachs See *von Sachs.*

Saussure See *de Saussure.*

Senebier, Jean (1779–1788) discovered that carbon dioxide is needed for *photosynthesis* and demonstrated this experimentally.

spectrum The band of colours that make up visible light (ie. red, orange, yellow, green, blue, violet). See *Chapter 4, Option, Communication, electromagnetic spectrum.*

thylakoids See *chloroplast.*

Tswett, Mikhail (1906) developed *chromatography* for separation of leaf pigments.

van Helmont, Johann (1630) The first studies of *photosynthesis* date back to 1630, when van Helmont showed that plants make their own organic matter and do not just absorb it from the soil. He weighed a pot of soil and a willow tree planted in it and showed that the plant increased its weight by 164 lb (approx. 70 kg) while the soil decreased in weight by a very small amount, one-eighth of a pound (about 0.05 kg). He incorrectly concluded that plant matter came from the water that he had added.

van Neil, Cornelius (1929) Research with certain bacteria showed that they use H_2S (hydrogen sulfide) instead of H_2O (water) in *photosynthesis*. These bacteria release S (sulfur) instead of O_2 (oxygen). Previously it was believed that that the O_2 produced in *photosynthesis* came from CO_2. Van Neil reasoned that as S was released from the H_2S in bacteria, the O_2 must be released from the H_2O in other plants. This was confirmed experimentally by *Ruben and Kamen.*

von Mayer, Julius Robert (1847) expressed the Law of Conservation of Energy which states that energy is not created or destroyed but changed from one form to another. He concluded that plants change the sun's energy to chemical energy in food (glucose).

von Sachs, Julius (1862) reported that starch appeared in leaves that photosynthesised. He identified *chlorophyll* in *chloroplasts* as the sites of glucose formation (ie. *photosynthesis*).